Lynn MacKaben Brown spent ten delightful years helping with her family's Christian bookstore before attending nursing school, eventually earning her M.A. with majors in nursing (teaching) and gerontology. She is a history columnist for SEG-Way News and has written for magazines as diverse as Moody Monthly, RN, Christian Communicator, and Toastmaster. She is a wife, mother, and grandmother.

This book is dedicated to my wonderful children: Peter, Rachel, Bethany, and Kirsten.

Lynn MacKaben Brown

CHRISTMAS CELEBRATION

AUSTIN MACAULEY PUBLISHERS™
LONDON • CAMBRIDGE • NEW YORK • SHARJAH

Copyright © Lynn MacKaben Brown 2021

All rights reserved. No part of this publication may be reproduced, distributed, or transmitted in any form or by any means, including photocopying, recording, or other electronic or mechanical methods, without the prior written permission of the publisher, except in the case of brief quotations embodied in critical reviews and certain other non-commercial uses permitted by copyright law. For permission requests, write to the publisher.

Any person who commits any unauthorized act in relation to this publication may be liable to criminal prosecution and civil claims for damages.

Ordering Information
Quantity sales: Special discounts are available on quantity purchases by corporations, associations, and others. For details, contact the publisher at the address below.

Publisher's Cataloging-in-Publication data
Brown, Lynn MacKaben
Christmas Celebration

ISBN 9781649792860 (Paperback)
ISBN 9781649792877 (Hardback)
ISBN 9781649792884 (ePub e-book)

Library of Congress Control Number: 2021921691

www.austinmacauley.com/us

First Published 2021
Austin Macauley Publishers LLC
40 Wall Street, 33rd Floor, Suite 3302
New York, NY 10005
USA

mail-usa@austinmacauley.com
+1 (646) 5125767

I am most grateful to Pastor Paul Berggren of Kenosha Bible Church and his Sixth Grade Pastor's Class which met every Saturday morning for three hours. And he gave tests! I am also grateful to the united parents who did not make this class optional and expected good grades. Later, I would discover that it was a level 100 theology class. In the meantime, the teaching and hundreds of memorized verses kept me from many sins and doubts. Thank you so much!

I also want to thank my Bible professors at Wheaton College, Moody Bible Institute, and Grace College for the knowledge they passed on and the skill of reading what is actually in the Bible, not what I thought was there or what I wanted to read.

I have also been blessed by extraordinary preachers in my home churches, at the Winona Lake Summer Conferences, and on WMBI, which was on constantly at my parents' house. My thanks to you all.

As to writing this book, I wish to thank Dr. Paulette Sauders, who was the first teacher to tell me that I was supposed to rewrite and edit my first drafts, even if they were A material. And thanks to Dr. Dennis E. Hensley, who taught me that "writing is rewriting as many times as it takes until it's the best you can write." Thank you to Liz Curtis Higgs. After a decade of struggle, I found my voice by reading Bad Girls of the Bible.

Finally, thanks to my family, with love, for being the guinea pigs of this devotional. Without our celebrations, this book would not have existed.

Christmas All Year—or Not

Welcome to my family's Christmas!

Wait. You want it to be *your* family's Christmas celebration. Let's discuss options.

When do you want to celebrate Christmas?

- Year-round: By celebrating Christmas on Sundays, you can rejoice forty-three weeks! Determine the Sunday before Christmas. That day you will read the Christmas devotional. Count back twenty-seven Sundays. That is your starting date. It will be near mid-June.
- Non-Advent Christmas Season: November 28 is the first day of daily devotions.
- Advent: Use the Advent Calendar in the following pages.

The ethnic celebrations I include are drawn from my own family heritage. I invite you to add yours. You could also add other countries to demonstrate that the gift of Jesus was for everyone in the world. If you do this, you will add a missionary flavor.

Make it *your* celebration.

- Decide if you want to sing, play an instrument, or listen to a recording of the music.
- Read the Bible version you prefer.
- If you have dietary restrictions, medical or religious or personal, feel free to replace food suggestions with festive ideas of your own.

It's fun to change your celebration! Don't feel that you must do every activity suggestion. Goodness! You would have to make three Christmas Eve dinners! Keep Christmas from becoming routine by selecting or inventing different celebrations.

It's fun to grow your celebration! You don't have to do all of the activities the first year. Your stress would skyrocket. Start with the elements most important to you and gradually add others that enhance the season. Consider giving up secular activities if stress mounts.

It's smart to store Christmas celebration items in an organized manner. Put away the articles in containers labeled with the day each item is to be used.

Most of all, be reverent and have fun. It's the birthday of the King of Kings!

Advent Week/Day		Page	Title
Advent Week 1: Hope			
Week1	Sunday	9	Despair and Hope
Week1	Monday	13	Christmas Math
Week1	Tuesday	16	Location, Location, Location
Week1	Wednesday	18	This is It!
Week1	Thursday	20	Incoming!
Week1	Friday	23	Unexpected Visitor
Week1	Saturday	26	An Excruciating Choice
Advent Week 2: Joy			
Week 2	Sunday	30	One More Joy
Week 2	Monday	32	But, Wait! There's More!
Week 2	Tuesday	34	Bah! Humbug!
Week 2	Wednesday	37	Good Question!
Week 2	Thursday	40	Girl Talk
Week 2	Friday	43	Mary's Praise
Week 2	Saturday	45	The Name Game
Advent Week 3: Peace			
Week 3	Sunday	47	Peace for Israel
Week 3	Monday	49	Paving the Road to Peace
Week 3	Tuesday	51	Peace for Joseph and Mary
Week 3	Wednesday	53	Personal Peace
Week 3	Thursday	56	Peace with God
Week 3	Friday	58	Peace with Others

Week 3	Saturday	60	Peace on Earth
Advent Week 4: Love (This is Christmas week. Use only enough devotions to get to the dated devotions.)			
Week 4	Sunday	62	Jesus Loves Us
Week 4	Monday	64	The Father Loves Us
Week 4	Tuesday	66	Returning the Love
December 22		67	Caesar's Census
December 23		70	Mystery Man
Christmas Eve		72	Journey to Bethlehem
Christmas Day		78	Christmas at Last!
December 26		83	The Black Sheep Gang
December 27		87	Birth Announcement
December 28		89	Rolling into Town
December 29		91	Spreading the Word
December 30		93	Officially Jewish
December 31		94	Purified and Redeemed
January 1		96	Simeon Speaks
January 2		98	Anna Announces
January 3		100	Stellar Announcement

January 4		103	When Herod Ain't Happy
January 5		107	Herod's Last Chance
January 6		110	Gifts Fit for a King
Bonus dated ethnic activities:			
December 6: Nicholas' Day		114	Generosity
December 13: Lucia's Day		116	Bringing God's Light to Others
January 13: Knut's Day		119	Final Birthday Bash for the King of kings!

Table of Contents

Despair and Hope	19
Christmas Math	24
Location, Location, Location	27
This Is It!	30
Incoming!	32
Unexpected Visitor	35
An Excruciating Choice	39
One More Joy	43
But, Wait! There's More!	45
Bah! Humbug!	47
Girl Talk	52
Mary's Praise	56
Name Game	59
Peace for Israel	62
Paving the Road to Peace	64
Peace for Joseph and Mary	66

Personal Peace	69
Peace with God	72
Peace with Others	74
Peace on Earth	76
Jesus Loves Us	78
The Father Loves Us	81
Returning the Love	83
Caesar's Census	85
Mystery Man	88
Journey to Bethlehem	90
Christmas at Last!	97
The Black Sheep Gang	102
Birth Announcement	106
Rolling into Town	108
Spreading the Word	111
Officially Jewish	113
Purified and Redeemed	115
Simeon Speaks	117
Anna Announces	119
Stellar Announcement	121
When Herod Ain't Happy	125
Herod's Last Chance	130
Gifts Fit for a King	133

Nicholas's Day December 6	137
Lucia's Day December 13	140
Knut's Day January 13	143

Despair and Hope

Read Isaiah 9:1–7

"Gloom, despair, and agony on me…"

Do you remember that comic song from the old television show *Hee Haw*? There's nothing funny, though, about those feelings in real life. Did you know that gloom and despair were why God invented Christmas?

Isaiah says, "Never mind the past. Okay, Naphtali and Zebulon were humbled by being dragged away into captivity with the other Lost Tribes of Israel. And, yes, before this prophecy is fulfilled, that same area will even be called Galilee of the Gentiles. That's right, I'm talking about that same land by the sea, along the Jordan. But listen up: there's hope!"

Hope! There's light at the end of the tunnel of gloom: hope for Jews physically separated from the temple of God, and hope for all of us separated from God by sin.

Hope in the Christian faith does not mean to wish, as in, "I hope I will get a doll for Christmas." It means looking toward something you really want and you know will come to pass. There's change in the wind? No more gloom and doom? Give me some of that hope!

Our Scripture then says that God will honor Galilee of the Gentiles.

Wait a minute. He humbled the area when it was Jewish and will honor it when it's overrun and even named for Gentiles? Jewish minds are aghast. What about dreams of political deliverance? How can this plan involve both Jews and Gentiles?

The rest of us impatiently push that idea aside. We want to know what will replace the gloom and despair. Listen to Isaiah. He's gushing. He's so excited, he can't get the words out fast enough.

1. Instead of walking in darkness, the people will be bathed in intense light.
   (That would be shocking and painful at first, but once your eyes adjust, you could see your world and your life for the first time.)
2. Even the shadow of death will shine! (It is the end of death.)
3. The nation of God will be enlarged. (Here's where Gentiles can join in.)
4. The joy of the people will increase.
5. There will be rejoicing: the crops are in and the battle is won. (That's intense Party Time!)
6. The people truly will be free.
7. War and oppression will be forever ended.

Who will make this happen? A person. His names describe who He is.

1. A Child: Jesus will be human, born like all humans.

2. A Son: Jesus will be the Son of God, a gift to us.
3. Governor: He will rule. It will be his responsibility.
4. Wonderful Counselor: He will show us how to live right.
5. Mighty God: He will have unlimited power and the absolute right to use it.
6. Everlasting Father: He will love us and provide for us.
7. Prince of Peace: He will lead us to inner peace which will result in external peace.

His kingdom will boundlessly increase his government, peace, physical expanse (David's throne and his kingdom), and justice and righteousness. It will last forever.

How can this be, in light of imperial conquests of the past and today's instability?

God will accomplish it. Enough said. Israel and the United States won't make it happen. All of the enemies of Israel can't stop it. The Ruler of All, the One with Infinite Might, has made it His personal mission. It will be done.

In one neat but exuberant package we have learned the why, who, and how of Christmas: Jesus the Messiah will vanquish gloom and despair with freedom and joy. The first step of the plan is His birth.

Questions to Consider:

1. What is the importance of prophecy?
2. Why is it important that prophecy be fulfilled precisely?

3. What do I look forward to the most in this coming kingdom time?
4. Which name of Jesus means the most to me today? Why?

Suggested prayer theme: Thank God for the name of Jesus that speaks most to me today, and for the kingdom he will establish.

Activity choices:

1. Music: "For Unto Us a Child Is Born" from *The Messiah*.
2. Begin an area to mount prophecies with today's prophecy in your favorite Bible version.
3. Begin an area to mount names of Jesus with those in today's reading.
4. Put out the Advent wreath or some other means of grouping the devotional candles. Light the candles each day during devotions.
5. Hang the Advent calendar that will be used beginning December 1. Explain to children how the calendar is used. I prefer one with biblical scenes.
6. Put a sunshine yellow candle in the Advent wreath. Leave the other holders empty.
7. Place candles of any color in your windows as a reminder to share the light of Jesus.
8. Decorate with sunshine yellow materials to mirror the Advent candle. In future weeks, you may use all colors together or dedicate a room to each color.

9. Dispense Swedish hospitality! Beginning today, everyone who comes to the door leaves with a treat. Drag them in for warmth, cookies and milk, or coffee and coffee cake. A proper Swedish housewife offers seven kinds of homemade cookies. Don't feel bad if you buy them instead. The hospitality is the point. You can also make it easier by using disposable cups and plates. I won't tell!

If you want to be really thoughtful, consider people with special needs, such as those who are gluten sensitive. The mailman and other delivery people can't stay, so prepare some drive-through goodies ahead of time using baggies and secure cup lids.

I have been known to run down the driveway after the FedEx man with a baggie of cookies shouting, "Stop! Stop!" The kids also found it fun to lie in wait for the mailman. Hospitality is fun!

Christmas Math

Read Daniel 9:24–27

"…Seven is the perfect number, we are told.
Let's be more like seven before we get too old…"
The Number Song by Ralph Carmichael

I hate math. For me, it ranks as a necessary evil right next to dentistry. However, my patients were certainly glad their nurse had mastered math skills when I administered medicine.

Yes, math is useful. Daniel used math to tell us exactly when Jesus would be born. However, like algebra, it takes some decoding. Come on, what fun is prophecy without mystery?

First, what is the timeline? We are told that it consists of events related to Jews and Jerusalem because Daniel, who receives the prophecy, was Jewish, although he lived far away from his home.

The key to decoding the timeline is the word seven. It is an actual number in this calculation, but seven also represents perfection in the sense of completion. Think of a circle. A circle, to be perfect, must be complete. God has determined this timeline, and it is perfect for the completion of His purposes, even if it seems excruciatingly long to us.

Fact 1: The Jewish timeline is "seventy 'sevens'" long. This is usually interpreted as 70 X 7 or 490 years.

Fact 2: The beginning of the timeline is a decree issued to restore and rebuild Jerusalem.

Fact 3: From then until the coming of the Anointed One, "seven 'sevens' and sixty-two sevens" will pass. This equals 483 years.

Fact 4: There were three decrees, none of which looked remotely likely at the time of this prophecy. The primary decree is usually dated as 457 B.C. When 483 years is added, we find the exact year that Jesus is baptized and is anointed by the Father with the Holy Spirit in the form of a dove, becoming the Anointed One. From there, we can count back to the year of his birth.

Fact 5: The Anointed One will be cut off and have nothing. So much for the physical kingdom the Jews expected.

Fact 6: Jerusalem and the temple will be destroyed. Therefore, the Anointed One can't appear after 70 A.D. when the Romans destroyed the city.

Fact 7: The last "seven" applies to the return of the Anointed One, the Second Coming.

For roughly four and a half centuries Jews waited for the birth of the Anointed one. For us, that's a long time to wait. But God waited for the perfect moment.

Question to consider:

When have I waited for God to answer prayer, only to realize afterward that He waited for that perfect moment?

Suggested Prayer Theme: Pray for perseverance while holding on to the prophecies of the return of the King.

Activity choices:

1. Music: "Come, Thou Long Expected Jesus."
2. Mount the prophecy with the prophecy collection.
3. Add the name Anointed One to the name collection.
4. Decorate the interior of your home with candles, preferably battery or electric candles.

Location, Location, Location

Read Micah 5:2–5

God sure wanted us to identify the Messiah. We've already looked at clues of why, who, what, and when. Verse 2 of this reading tells us where to find him. The ruler, the Messiah, will come from Bethlehem. But what is Ephrathah?

In Genesis 48:7 Jacob's wife Rachel's burial is located near Ephrath (that is, Bethlehem). Ephrathah is another form of Ephrath. God wanted it understood exactly where His Son was to be born: the city related to David and Rachel.

God doesn't fudge on his promises. Of all the towns in the world, tiny Bethlehem was exactly where Jesus was born. God didn't say, "Oh, well, Jerusalem is close enough. After all, David ruled there." God always fulfills prophecy precisely.

Here's something interesting. The ruler's "origins are from old, from ancient times." Origins? More than one? That's strange. It's the key to show us that "old" and "ancient" are a parallelism: thoughts that are similar but different in an important way.

Let's see. If Bethlehem is related to David, the ruler has an origin in the ruling line of David, who is definitely "old" news. But "ancient" is long before that. Even in the first times, when time had appeared as a new concept in eternity, this ruler's origin was already planted. That could only be God.

This ruler, this Messiah, who will come out of Bethlehem will rule by virtue of being both the Son of David and the Son of God.

Question to consider:

As a child of God, I am to be like him. When I make a promise, do I fulfill it exactly or do I fudge in favor of my convenience?

Suggested Prayer Theme: Pray for steadfastness to keep promises wholeheartedly.

Activity choices:

1. Music: "O Little Town of Bethlehem"
2. Put out a set of Bethlehem buildings. Make it the center of your Christmas set. What?
   Your crèche doesn't have more than the stable? Have fun adding to your set! In future years you may want to upgrade, but for now, make it a family art project! Use cardboard boxes or wooden blocks or Legos or Lincoln Logs or—if you are ambitious—gingerbread!
3. Put up Christmas lights inside your house. Our living room is decorated as a garden room so we have white lights near the ceiling all year. During the Christmas season, they are Christmas lights.

They are "fireflies" the rest of the year and great mood lighting!

This Is It!

Read Isaiah 7:14

We have seen how God told us about the birth of Jesus through prophecy. He told us who, what, when, where, and why. He also told us how. This verse in Isaiah gave us a sign pointing directly to the Messiah: he would be the one born of a virgin. This did not mean she would be a virgin when she married or that she would be a young, married woman, as the Jews interpreted it. That would be no prophecy at all. It happened all the time.

We are so used to the idea of the virgin birth that it hardly phases us today. But take a moment to think of it. Really think about it, as if you had never heard of it before. It's amazing! It's miraculous! Imagine a huge neon sign with an arrow pointing to the pregnant Mary: THIS IS IT!

And even while we think of this human girl, we see that she calls him Immanuel, which means "God with us." Since his formal name is Jesus, perhaps Immanuel was a nickname or a name used only in the family. I hope not! Can you imagine the reaction of siblings? Maybe it was Mary's secret name for Jesus, since it says *she* called him that.

The result of the virgin birth is a boy who is fully human but also fully God. Only God would have thought of something like that!

Question to consider:

What practical result in my life results from realizing that Jesus is "God with us?"

Suggested Prayer Theme: Pray for constant awareness that God is with me.

Activity choices:

1. Music: "O Come, O Come, Emmanuel"
2. Add the name Emmanuel or Immanuel to the name posting area.
3. Switch on your outside Christmas lighting. Share more than the hope of prophecy with your neighbors. Share Jesus!

Incoming!

Read Luke 1:11–17, then Micah 4:5–6.

Let's jump to prophecies made shortly before the birth of Jesus. They are all delivered by angels. "Angel" simply means "messenger."

The celestial species we usually call angels is not the girly, soft, fluffy image of our Christmas decorations. Angels are always spoken of as "he," and they are the servants and soldiers of God, always ready to take a message, protect a child, or do battle with the enemy. Perhaps we could think of angels as God's Delta Force.

Their appearance and force of personality is such that every time they appear, people nearby are scared out of their wits, unless the angels alter their appearance to resemble humans.

Imagine yourself in Zechariah's sandals. You're alone at church, serving in your usual capacity. Perhaps you are setting up chairs for the service or preparing to teach. In the next heartbeat a Delta Force soldier in full battle array is standing next to you. Would you be stunned and terrified? You bet your sweet sandals!

Zechariah is old. Wouldn't you think the angel would appear as a non-threatening human? That would be surprising enough. After all, we're in heart attack territory. At least the angel says immediately, "Don't be afraid." Yeah, right.

Zechariah is a priest, an upright man, who has stopped believing in miracles and in the power of prayer. The angel is like Marley's ghost shouting at Scrooge: "Man of the worldly mind, do you believe in me or not?" Zechariah is too scared even to say Scrooge's line, "I do! I must."

Once Zechariah believes that angels still walk the earth and speak with men, he can again believe that anything is possible with God. What is the message? Zechariah will have a child. Not just a child, but a son. And not just any son. He will be the only human to be filled with the Holy Spirit *even from birth*. I have no idea what that means, but the idea is astounding.

The Messiah will soon be among us and Zechariah's son will be his town crier. "Make way for the king!"

Questions to consider:

How would I react if I were Zechariah?

Do I really believe that miracles happen today? In the power of prayer?

If I were told by God that Jesus was returning in a year, how would my life change?

Suggested prayer theme: Pray to live as if the date of Jesus's return was known and imminent.

Activity choices:

1. Music: "Prepare Ye the Way of the Lord" from John Peterson's *Night of Miracles* or "Every Valley Shall Be Exalted" from *The Messiah*.

2. Set out Jerusalem buildings including the temple ten kilometers north of your Bethlehem village. Obviously, I don't mean the distance literally, but it is important to visualize relative distances between locations in the future. Ten kilometers is quite close.

3. Place Zechariah and an angel in the Jerusalem temple. You don't have a Zechariah figure? Use any figure/doll the right size or connect a Styrofoam ball and cone then dress it in robe and headwear.

4. Add the title The Lord Your God to the name collection.

5. Mount angels on your walls.

6. Draw your version of a Delta Force angel.

Unexpected Visitor

Read Luke 1:26–33.

Mary is alone. We don't know where she is, but she's probably at home. Mary is industriously cooking or cleaning house. Perhaps she's also singing a psalm.

Suddenly, she is aware of a stranger at the door. He doesn't look or dress strangely. (After all, we don't read that Mary was terrified of him.) Mary cleans her hands on a wet rag and approaches the stranger to offer hospitality.

Her mind runs over reasons why the stranger may have come to her. In her small town, she knows everyone.

When a stranger comes to my home, he needs directions, is selling something, or is trying to convert me to his religion. Mary's mind is probably running over the first two options.

The stranger greets Mary with odd but powerful words. The words upset Mary. Whatever happened to good old "Hello?" What would your reaction be? What would you say? I'd react the same way as Mary: stunned silence.

Let's think about that greeting. To be favored by a king is to be given special, personal attention. Something draws his notice: perhaps a glorious battle triumph, maybe meritorious service in civil affairs, or it could be some outstanding proof of loyalty. Or, like David and Mephibosheth, it could be merely the needy son of an old friend. Most likely, what drew God's interest to Mary was her character and her devotion.

Please don't get the idea that Mary *deserved* to be the mother of Jesus. Then we are not talking about a favor, but a reward. A favor is something given from the generosity of the king. Mary, herself, understood that obeying God was only what she owed him. It was because of this humility that Gabriel's words troubled her. Not only was she to be favored, she was to be *highly* favored. Mary couldn't even guess what that meant.

"The Lord is with you, Mary." We skip over this so glibly! Stop. Think. This is not the usual greeting of "The Lord be with you." This is not some nebulous theological statement that Mary already knows from Scripture. This is a statement of fact. The Lord is present with you, Mary, right here, right now.

After calming her fears, Gabriel announces the birth of the Messiah, referring to prophecy that Mary will recognize. The angel then gives Mary specific direction to name the baby Jesus. This is odd for several reasons:

1. Normally, the father named the child not the mother. Okay, we can stretch the point because God is the baby's father, but the locals won't understand.
2. Children were traditionally named after relatives.
3. The name Jesus is Greek, not Jewish. We know, of course, that this indicates his international mission,

but from Mary's point of view the command was odd.

This is Jesus's birth announcement. Today, doctors or even discount pregnancy tests give us the good news. Not quite the pizzazz, is it?

Question to consider:

If God asked me to do something that seemed odd, would I do it?

Suggested prayer theme: Pray to obey the will of God regardless of what that might be.

Activity choices:

1. Music: "Mary, Did You Know?"
2. Add Son of the Most High to the name collection.
3. Remove Zechariah and the angel from the temple. Previous figures should always be removed unless otherwise stated.
4. Put the Nazareth set north and slightly east of Jerusalem and set it in the hills. A shallow bowl could represent the surrounding hills.
5. Add Mary and Gabriel in her home.
6. Put out all the rest of your angel decorations, even those that will go on the tree later.
7. Put out a "manger" and a small mound of straw. Your crèche manger is hopefully too small for this activity.

Explain the manger to children like this: "As we prepare to welcome Jesus into the world, let's use this manger as a reminder to do good deeds as gifts for Him. Every time we do an act of devotion, such as reading the Bible, praying, or attending a church service, put one piece of straw into the manger. Also put one in for every good deed you do. That includes reminding someone else to put his or her straw in the manger. But remember, God doesn't want us to boast about our good deeds in front of others, so sneak the straw into the manger when no one is looking! Let's see how soft a bed. we can make for Jesus by midnight, Christmas morning!"

An Excruciating Choice

Read Matthew 1:18–21.

> Two roads diverged in a yellow wood,
> And sorry I could not travel both
> And be one traveler, long I stood…
>> "The Road Not Taken" by Robert Frost

Joseph never thought, he would be in this quandary. Mary is pregnant. He knows he isn't the child's father. Mary's story that she is pregnant by God is just too much to believe. But she never lies. And her eyes show earnest truthfulness. Day after day he struggles with a decision. Night after night he tosses in bed.

But why is Joseph's struggle so difficult? They're not married yet. What's the real problem here? Marry her or abandon her.

Not so fast. The situation is much more complicated than that.

The first problem was legal. In that day, a pledge was a contract. It was not like an American engagement today, which is only the promise of intention to marry. The pledge exchanged between Mary and Joseph was so strong that they were considered already united. That is why Joseph is called Mary's husband. If so, however, what was the purpose of the pledge period? That's when the man prepared their home, the wedding was planned, and all of the invited relatives and guests made or bought wedding presents.

Joseph's next problem was spiritual. Since, he believed that Mary had committed adultery, he was forced to choose between God, who said that he was not to marry a woman who had committed adultery, and Mary, whom he loved so much that it hurt! We know he loved her intensely or he would not have struggled so hard with his decision. Joseph chose God.

Now, Joseph had to work through an ethical struggle: justice vs. mercy. Mosaic Law demanded death for adultery. With Rome reserving the death penalty to itself, that could not be carried out except for a clandestine honor killing. What was usually done was to drag the adulterer into a public area and stone her, just short of death. Of course, there were accidents…

Joseph could also divorce Mary publicly by declaring the reason why the contract was broken. This would ruin Mary's reputation. No decent man would marry her. She would be an outcast from society. Every ounce of mercy and love in Joseph was repulsed by the idea.

So, Joseph toyed with the idea of a private solution. I would like to know, how he thought, he could have a private divorce so she wouldn't be publicly disgraced. Nazareth was a town where everybody knew everyone else, and many of them were related.

If you've lived in a small town, you know what the gossip mill is like. Joseph and Mary not getting married after all, plus Mary obviously being pregnant... If you haven't lived in a small town, but you've seen *My Big, Fat Greek Wedding*, imagine trying to arrange a secret divorce with families like that on both sides! Even moving to another town wouldn't solve the problem. Family would be sure to visit.

Whatever Joseph was considering, it was ripping him apart. That's when an angel appeared. This time it was an unnamed angel, and he appeared in a dream instead of reality. Why? I don't know.

As usual, every word of the prophecy is important. In addressing him by name, Joseph knows the message is specifically for him. Son of David reminds Joseph that he is prophetically eligible for the role of *legal* father of the Messiah.

Notice what frightens Joseph. He's not afraid of the angel nor of the message. He is afraid of displeasing God by wedding Mary. Wow.

Joseph has the answer to his dilemma, but he's wondering how this can please God. The angel kindly explains: Mary really is pregnant by the Holy Spirit. She is telling the truth. Joseph sighs with relief. Mary is the girl he always believed her to be.

Next, a partnership is announced: Mary will give birth to a son and Joseph will name him Jesus. Why Jesus? Because it means "Savior." And now Joseph can barely breathe: he, a mere carpenter, will be the legal father of the Messiah!

I'm sure all Joseph could think about when he awakened was that God had arranged that he could both please God and have Mary. He has hope again!

And now, the stage is set. The events are about to come into alignment.

Questions to consider:

One of Joseph's struggles was between the two greatest commandments: Love God and love others as yourself. Was there a time when I struggled to reconcile these commandments? Consider how I resolved it. Was it the right thing to do?

Joseph's other struggle was balancing justice and mercy. How is my balance? Do I err on one side or the other repeatedly? How can I become better balanced?

Suggested prayer theme: Pray for wisdom to balance between justice and mercy in all situations.

Activity choices:

1. Music: "A Child of Hope" from *It's the Lord's Thing* musical by Lani Smith.
2. Place Joseph and the angel in his house in Nazareth.
3. Add all hanging angels to lamp knobs, cabinet knobs, anywhere else.

One More Joy

Read Luke 1:5–10.

We've been talking about hope. Now, let's talk about the joy of Christmas. In fact, let's look again at the story of Zechariah and the joy that came before Christmas.

Zechariah and Elizabeth already had all kinds of joy:

1. They were both of the priestly line.
2. Through obedience, they enjoyed the closest relationship possible with God, with the exception of the prophets—and there had not been one of those for four hundred years.
3. They loved each other very much. This is implied because they were still married after decades of childlessness although barrenness was grounds for divorce.
4. On this day, Zechariah was serving in the temple. He had been chosen "by lot" to burn incense on the altar. "By lot" is similar to throwing dice, but before Pentecost God often showed his will in this way. The burning of incense was an honor many priests never were chosen to perform.

Incense represented the prayers of the people who were praying outside. The chosen priest symbolically brought the people's prayers before God. Zechariah and Elizabeth had prayed for decades for one more element of joy: a child. That prayer would be granted as part of the Christmas story.

Question to consider:

Zechariah and Elizabeth were now old. They had prayed many years for a child. Do I show this persistence in prayer?

Suggested prayer theme: Pray for persistence in prayer.

Activity choices:

1. Music: "Carol of the Bells." Accompany it with any bells you have on hand.
2. Return Zechariah to the temple in Jerusalem.
3. Decorate your home with the traditional green of Christmas without removing the yellow décor. The green represents joy and everlasting life because evergreens don't die during winter. It also represents good fortune. Think of the shamrock. Jesus's birth certainly represents all of these things.

a. Add a green candle to the Advent wreath or candle group.
b. Decorate with evergreen wreaths and boughs.
c. Erect your Christmas tree this week unless you will be planting it.

But, Wait! There's More!

Read Luke 1:11–17, then Ephesians 3:20–21.

What is the first thing the angel says after, "Don't be afraid?" He says, "Your prayer has been heard." I'm sure Elizabeth's prayer has also been heard, but the angel is dealing with a priest who no longer believes in prayer. We'll see that next time when we look at Zechariah's reaction.

If he no longer believes in prayer and the couple is old, when was this prayer uttered? It's probable that Zechariah's prayers on this subject ceased many years ago, but that made no difference to God. He heard the prayer request and understood the faith exhibited at that time. However, he waited (as he always does) for the perfect moment. That was now.

But, wait! There's more! This is the whole gift package:

1. A child
2. A son to carry on the lineage
3. Your (beloved) wife Elizabeth will bear him. No second wife needed.
4. The son will delight his father. He's guaranteed not to be a lazy, godless ingrate.
5. His birth will bring rejoicing to many people.

6. God will see him as great. Remember, the angel is talking to a priest.
7. The Holy Spirit will fill him from birth.
8. Many Jews will return to God because of him.
9. He will be the forerunner of the Messiah.

Question to consider:

When has God given me overwhelmingly more than I asked for?

Prayer theme suggestion: Thank God for His overwhelming generosity.

Activity choices:

1. Add the angel in the temple.
2. Music: "Ring the Bells" accompanied by bells.
3. Hand bells on doors opening outside.

Bah! Humbug!

Read Luke 1:18–25.

Well, if it isn't old Scrooge and his "Bah! Humbug!" attitude. After an announcement of the miracle pregnancy personally delivered by Gabriel, Zechariah responds with the equivalent of, "Yeah? Prove it!" What skepticism! What cynicism!

Was this really a miracle pregnancy? Oh, yes. Remember, Dr. Luke is writing this, and he tells us in the beginning of his book that he carefully researched everything. Dr. Luke knows how childbirth works. This isn't it.

Gabriel says, "Okay, since you won't believe an angel, believe your own mouth. You will be mute until this son is born." Does this mean it's not permissible to ask God questions? Not at all. It was Zechariah's unbelief and bad attitude that resulted in this punishment.

The people waiting for Zechariah wondered what was taking so long. All he had to do was burn some incense. When he returned unable to speak, they immediately knew that he'd had an encounter with God or angels. They couldn't understand what he was trying to tell them, but the stage was set for the future. There was great awe and curiosity.

And, then, there was Elizabeth. We don't know her immediate response when her husband arrived home mute, but with an astounding story. We do know her response after she realized she was pregnant.

What she did: she stayed at home seeing no one but her husband for five months. Why? We're not told. Maybe she just wanted to hug the wonderful news to herself for a while until the pregnancy was so obvious, that no one could doubt it.

Elizabeth recognized that God's gift was *for her*. She knew the gift wasn't just for Zechariah. She also knew God could have chosen any Jewish woman, but he had chosen her. Elizabeth tells us what this gift means to her.

1. It was a sign of God's favor. Quite possibly, Elizabeth had been torturing herself with the thought she was barren because of some sin she hadn't recognized. This pregnancy showed her that she was on good terms with God.
2. God took away the disgrace of barrenness. People had talked, and it had hurt Elizabeth. Barrenness brought more shame than anything except flagrant sin or loathsome disease. It was an acceptable reason for divorce, hands down. In fact, some rabbis even said it was the husband's duty to divorce a barren wife and marry again to carry on the family name.

Three different reactions to the same situation: Zechariah, the people at the temple, and Elizabeth. But by the end of this reading, even Zechariah believed. He had no choice. The proof was blooming before his eyes.

Do you think he has joy now?

Questions to consider:

How would I have reacted to the news?

Have I ever become cynical or skeptical when God's answers to prayer don't run on my timetable?

Suggested prayer theme: Pray to accept God's timetable for events and answers to prayer.

Activity choices:

1. Leave Zechariah and the angel in the temple.
2. Music: "Ring Out Ye Wild and Merry Bells"
3. Make a Thanksgiving Bell Garland for your wall.
4. Cut out bells and write a praise on each one. Mount them on the wall in a continuous strand. Add to the garland throughout the season.

Good Question!

Read Luke 1:26–38.

The same angel who spoke to Zechariah brings another proclamation of a miraculous birth, but what a different response!

Mary is humble at the greeting, then believing. She, too, asks a question, but because of her belief the asking is not considered presumptuous. She believes she will become pregnant. She just wants to know how it's going to happen. By her question, Mary obviously knows the facts of life.

The angel answers her and volunteers the happy news that her much older cousin Elizabeth is now also pregnant.

Mary humbly accepts the assignment as the mother of the Messiah. She sees herself as God's servant. That was the highest relationship available at that time and available only to Jews. It is her recognition of this relationship that is the basis of Mary's humility. She doesn't think she's doing anything great by obeying God. It is merely her servant duty to her King.

It's important to note that God does not force her to be the mother of Jesus. He waits for her agreement. This is how God deals with us: he respects the personal will he created within us.

Let's look at some details. The angel tells Mary that her son will inhabit King David's throne, as prophesied. Luke writes a genealogy of Jesus when telling of His baptism, proving Jesus's right to the throne by *birth* through Mary. Matthew begins his gospel with Joseph's genealogy, proving that Jesus also had the *legal* right to the throne through Joseph.

Now, let's look at some dates. It is now the sixth month of the Jewish calendar, which is August–September for us. Elizabeth is in her sixth month, so we can conclude she became pregnant in the twelfth month of the Jewish calendar, or February–March to us. If John was born full-term, his birthday lay in the ninth month of Kislev, or November–December to us.

If Mary became pregnant when she received the announcement from the angel, which seems probable, Jesus would be born in Sivan, or May–June. During Sivan, Jews celebrate the Festival of Weeks or the Festival of New

Grain. It is an offering of the first grain of the fields. To Christians, this has become the time of Pentecost.

There are parallels between Jesus and the Festival of Weeks. Jesus begins the harvesting of souls for the kingdom of God. The sacrifices of the festival are bread—think of the Last Supper—and two animal offerings: one for sin, the other for fellowship. The animal sacrifices foreshadowed Jesus's work: dying for our sins and reinstating fellowship with God.

What joy Mary had! She was the mother of the Messiah!

Questions to consider:

Would I react like Mary, knowing I would be the target of gossip and slander?

Do I ask God questions? Are they inquisitive or impertinent?

Do I really believe that nothing is impossible with God?

Suggested prayer theme: Pray to acquire a humble heart like Mary.

Activity choices:

1. Put Mary in her house in Nazareth with the angel.
2. Music: "Nothing is Impossible"
3. Music: "Ding, Dong Merrily on High" while decorating the interior of the house with bells

Girl Talk

Read Luke 1:39−45.

At the time of the angel's announcement to Mary. Mary *hurried* to Elizabeth's house.

Why did she hurry? We're not told, but my guess is that Mary immediately informed her mother and Joseph about the angel's visit and this was the result of those conversations. Mary was packed off before her pregnancy showed so the family could decide what to do.

Mary was in turmoil. She was full of joy because she believed the angel. She was not naïve so she understood the upheaval she had injected into the family and her insecure future, humanly speaking. No one believed her. Where could she turn? She clutched onto the angel's words. Cousin Elizabeth is also miraculously pregnant. She will understand.

Mary began the long journey to Elizabeth's home, desperately needing someone to believe and support her. Elizabeth was a godly woman and may have had a reputation for loving and supporting others. She was much older and could give the love and support of a grandmother.

Luke sticks resolutely to critical facts and, therefore, tells nothing of the journey. Mary would have traveled with a group that included men for protection from highway robbers. Most likely the group would have been family. Perhaps even Joseph traveled with her, since; we don't know where he was when the angel spoke to him. The family was poor. Everyone walked. No donkey.

From Nazareth in northern Galilee, Mary climbed over the bowl of hills, crossed the Jordan River and traveled through Perea because no decent Jew would travel through Samaria. Then she re-crossed the river and climbed into Judean hill country. Other than the arid Jordan weather, the walk would have been pleasant in the height of summer: dry with day temperatures in the mid-eighty-degree range.

Luke skips all this and gets right to the meeting of the expectant mothers. When Elizabeth hears Mary's greeting three things happened: (1) Baby John jumped for joy, (2) Elizabeth, the priestly descendent, was filled with the Holy Spirit, and (3) Elizabeth prophesied.

Before Pentecost, the Holy Spirit only filled the rare individual for a specific mission. Female prophets were extremely rare. In addition, Elizabeth is the first or second prophet in four hundred years! (We'll meet Anna later.) All of this would not have been lost on Mary.

The prophecy serves three purposes: (1) It is another testimony to the deity of Jesus. (2) It is a welcome confirmation to Mary. (3) Elizabeth first learns of Mary's wonderful secret in this way. Remember, Elizabeth didn't know. Considering the state of communication back then, it's probable that Elizabeth didn't even know Mary was coming.

Elizabeth pronounces three blessings: (1) Mary is the most blessed of women. (2) Her child will be blessed. (3)

Mary, the believer, is blessed. Mary's blessedness is related to Jesus and to her belief, not to her own merit.

As Christians, we need to find a healthy balance in our thoughts of Mary. Protestants often emphasize her humanity and this is appropriate. But it is important to recognize her unique status given by God's favor. She is blessed as no one else will ever be.

On the other hand, Elizabeth, who is the first to believe Mary and recognize her unique status, treats her as a kinswoman. Elizabeth does not genuflect to Mary, nor does she pray to her, nor invoke her help as an intercessor with God.

Have you noticed the repetition of threes? (1) Three things happen at Mary's greeting. (2) Elizabeth speaks a prophecy with three outcomes. (3) Elizabeth pronounces three blessings.

Three is the number of God, most notably the trinity. And the trinity is here. God the Father oversees and orders all things. Jesus is in Mary's uterus. The Holy Spirit fills Elizabeth and originates the prophecy she speaks.

Truly, God is in these events.

Questions to consider:

Who has encouraged me in ministry when others discouraged me or times were difficult?

Am I the kind of person to whom others flee when their worlds are turned upside down?

Is there someone I should encourage in his or her ministry today?

Suggested prayer theme: Thank God for people who have encouraged me in my ministry throughout the years.

Activity Choices:

1. Put Elizabeth in her house in the Judean hills. Move Mary from her house over the hills and into Perea to avoid Samaria then back across the Jordan River and up the hills to Elizabeth's house.
2. Music: "I Heard the Bells on Christmas Day"
3. Eat sugar cookie bells!
4. Begin collecting baby items for poor mothers and infants in your church or a Christian pregnancy center in honor of Mary and Elizabeth. When you give a party ask each guest to bring one item.

Mary's Praise

Read Luke 1:46–56.

This scripture passage is traditionally called The Magnificat and is referred to as a song. It is possible, since it includes Psalm 103:17 and Psalm 107:9. However, the Bible says Mary *said* the words. Either way, Mary was a poet. It's evident she knew Scripture well. Look, how she slipped those verses into the poem!

Had she been working on this while traveling or was it a spontaneous burst of joy and gratitude? I vote for the latter. Maybe God had a direct hand in it, too.

I once sang a well-known gospel song as a solo, but when I began to sing the third verse my mind went blank. With an attitude of "the show must go on," I continued to sing and was amazed by the words coming out of my mouth: a completely new verse with the rhyme and style of the original song! Those words touched more hearts than any other performance I have given as a soloist.

Let's get back to Mary's poem. The contents are self-explanatory. Mary begins with the purpose of the poem and why she is creating it, then lists six things God has done for which she praises him. Mary refers to God as "my Savior." If she said "the Savior" instead, the doctrine of the

Immaculate Conception could survive this scripture passage, although it would still fail logically. But Mary says "*my* savior" during the first seven lines that refer to herself. Only beginning with line eight does her poem extend to other people.

Mary stayed with Elizabeth for about three months—probably until the birth of John. What a joy it would have been to celebrate with Zechariah and Elizabeth, and hold the one who would prepare the way for her own child!

Mary's return to Nazareth in her fourth month was not as pleasant. It was during the cool, rainy, winter season with day temperatures in the fifties. But by now Joseph had probably seen the angel. If he was not traveling with Mary, he would have hastened to her as soon as he heard she was coming. And that would have made the miserable trip better than a jaunt to the Riviera.

Questions to consider:

Do I know Scripture as well as Mary did?

When have I been so full of joy I could have burst? How did I celebrate?

What has God done for me that gives me deep, heartfelt joy?

Prayer theme suggestion: Praise God for what he has done that gives me effusive joy.

Activity choices:

1.   Keep Mary and Elizabeth in the house of the latter.
2.   Music: "Caroling, Caroling"

3. Write a poem of praise to God. Don't worry if it's not publishable. It's between you and God. Do the best you can.
4. Put bells on all of your pets.
5. Bell Pudding: Make pudding with a bell hidden in it. It is said that the one who finds the bell in his serving will have a joyous New Year. (Warn eaters so they will be careful. Do not do this with small children, of course.)

Name Game

Read Luke 1:57–66.

In the Jewish month relating to our November–December, a huge block party pulsated in and around the home of Zechariah and Elizabeth. The miracle baby was born! All of the neighbors and family members came to celebrate.

I'm sure more people than Doctor Luke were amazed that elderly Elizabeth had not only conceived, she had the "young" internal organs and the endurance to survive labor and delivery. The men probably joked with Zechariah about his elderly prowess and asked how many more children he would have.

During the circumcision celebration, when the baby was welcomed into the Jewish nation, *they* (whoever *they* were) wanted to name him after Zechariah, but Elizabeth spoke up and insisted on the name John. *They* completely missed the meaning of the name: Yahweh (God's personal name) is gracious. Grace is getting what you don't deserve. The world certainly didn't deserve Jesus.

Elizabeth was "only a woman" so they asked the father, what name he wanted. Since they made signs to him, Zechariah was apparently deaf as well as mute: an interesting comment on his spiritual state during the angel's visit.

Zechariah wrote, "His name *is* John" implying the baby was already named—and he was. At that point of obedience, Zechariah discovered he could speak. He began praising God.

The neighbors were awed. We use that word so sloppily. Stop a few moments and consider its depth of meaning.

They named the baby John and spread the story throughout the hill country of Judea. Everywhere people talked about John and wondered what he would become. Interesting. I'm sure Zechariah told them.

Somehow, the Holy Spirit's influence on John made a difference so significant and obvious that all Judea expected him to be someone special.

They were right.

Questions to consider:

Have I ever been disobedient but later had the chance to do right: a do-over? Did I choose correctly the next time?

Suggested prayer theme: Thank and praise God for the mercy of second chances.

Activity choices:

1. Place Zechariah and Elizabeth in their home.
2. Music: "Go Tell It on the Mountain." Yes, I know this is about Jesus, but John is the herald of Jesus and will tell that the Messiah is coming.
3. Since the joy of Zechariah and Elizabeth spread throughout Judea, let's spread cheer. Decorate your

vehicles (bikes, cars, trucks) with streamers and bells!

Peace for Israel

Read Luke 1:67–75.

This third week of celebration is centered on peace. We need it after the tumultuous events of the previous weeks! Unless you are using this as a year-long celebration, you are in the press of the Christmas season with less than two weeks until Christmas Day.

Today's reading is just a continuation of yesterday's scripture passage and probably occurred the same day.

Whew! Talk about a run-on sentence! The entire poem is futuristic, looking forward to the Second Coming. Even the child that is now within Mary does not become Israel's salvation until then.

How does this tie into Christmas? Because without the first advent, which we celebrate at Christmas, there would be no second advent. The final and lasting peace of Israel is tied to Christmas.

I know. I thought it rather odd, too, but there it is.

Question to consider:

Do I pray for peace for Jerusalem, as commanded in Psalm 122:6?

Suggested prayer theme: Pray for peace for Jerusalem.

Activity choices:

1. Leave Zechariah in his house, but remove Elizabeth.
2. Add a medium blue candle to your arrangement.
3. Music: "Shalom." Sing it in a round if you can!
4. Decorate with the leaves of a fig tree (real or paper) and/or the Israeli flag which are symbols of Israel.
5. Eat figs, a "figgy pudding," or something else containing figs.

Paving the Road to Peace

Read Luke 1:76-80.

Today, we are finishing the prophecy of Zechariah. Incidentally, Zechariah and Elizabeth are the only husband and wife prophets!

This part of the prophecy clearly links John with Jesus. John will prepare the way for Jesus's ministry by giving people the knowledge that salvation is possible through the forgiveness of sins because of God's mercy. Mercy means *not* getting what we deserve: the full judgment for our sins.

God's mercy is the link. It is that which causes Jesus, the Prince of Peace to come from heaven and shine on all the people of the world. The purpose of his coming is direct us to the way of peace.

We have not been able to find our way, even with the Scriptures, so God mercifully sent us a guide. If we walk in his footsteps, we will have peace. You see, peace is not a one-time thing. It is a way of life.

Questions to consider:

Am I willing to follow Jesus in the Path of Peace regardless of where it goes?

Suggested prayer theme: Pray for sensitivity to the guidance of the Holy Spirit and willingness to follow Jesus.

Activity choices:

1. Keep Zechariah in his home.
2. Music: "(I'm Following Jesus) One Step at a Time," especially the verse that talks of peace
3. Signify the Path of Peace in some way

   a. Decorate an existing path.
   b. Go outside and leave a path of birdseed.
   c. Eat a cake/cookie decorated with a "path."
   d. Solve a maze puzzle on paper or by video game.

4. Follow a path in some way

   a. Play Fox and Geese in the snow.
   b. Follow a path in the wild.
   c. Use a maze of sidewalks for a treasure hunt. Clues tell the path to take to the treasure by indicating choices at sidewalk junctions.
   d. Walk a meditation labyrinth.

Peace for Joseph and Mary

Read Matthew 1:18–25

Once again, we are revisiting a reading. We have returned to Joseph, who has been working and worrying in Nazareth while Mary has been visiting with Elizabeth. We don't know when his angel dream occurred, but it was sometime after Mary told him. Mary may have returned to Nazareth by now, her pregnancy hidden by loose robes, or she may still be with Elizabeth.

We've already looked at the angel's visit. The next section records that this is prophecy fulfilled. We're interested in the last section: Joseph's response. He now had a clear course of action from God, and he immediately acts upon it. He brings Mary home as his wife. They live as a married couple, except there is no sex for the six months until the birth of Jesus. Now, that's a man with self-control!

Why is this reading in the week dedicated to peace? Because Joseph now has personal peace. His dilemma is finally resolved. He is at peace with God and can still have Mary. Mary is also at peace with God. Where there was friction because of Joseph's conflict, all is now at peace between the spouses.

When a man and woman each love and serve God, they will be drawn closer to one another.

Questions to consider:

If I am married or engaged, how would I rate my love and dedication to God?

How would I rate my partner's relationship with God?

Suggested prayer theme: Pray for the relationship of each partner to God. If unmarried, pray for your future partner, if you hope to have one.

Activity choices:

1. Place Joseph in his home.
2. Music: "Where the Spirit of the Lord Is, There is Peace"
3. Experiment with triangles

   a. Draw a triangle with all sides equal, sitting on a side. The height of the triangle indicates devotion to God of each spouse (side). The base side represents peace and unity between the spouses.
   b. Draw a triangle with more height than width. As devotion to God by each spouse increases, what happens to their relationship with each other?
   c. Draw a triangle with a wider baseline. Now draw one side steeply upward representing one spouse with a close relationship to God. Make the other side a much narrower angle, representing a spouse who is not devoted to

God or is an unbeliever. The second spouse jeopardizes their relationship to God as a couple and they are farther apart in the marriage. It's sad.

    d. Draw the shape that represents you and your spouse or fiancé, if you have one.

4. Decorate your house with the most desirable triangle. Isn't it interesting that it's the shape of a Christmas tree?

Personal Peace

Read John 14:27, II Thessalonians 3:16, Philippians 4:6–7.

After the hustle and bustle of angel appearances and miracle pregnancies, we enter into a time of tranquility between Mary's fourth and ninth month of pregnancy. Joseph and Mary are home together in Nazareth facing the gossipers, but at peace because they know they are in God's will.

During this peaceful time, we will look at some Scriptures that describe various kinds of peace that make up the path of peace on which Jesus guides us. Of course, Jesus first had to be born, so these are all the result of Christmas.

Let's begin by looking at personal peace. Jesus spoke what is recorded in John 14:27 shortly before his death. It has a poetic feel because every sentence is composed of two similar but slightly different phrases, much like Jewish poetry.

In the first sentence, Jesus says it's not just any peace but *my peace*. It's not just left; it is a precious gift. The world gives gifts with an eye toward profit and usually expects a gift in return. Jesus gives peace freely and simply out of love. He will never take it away.

The last sentence is a pair of commands. Although Jesus will never take back the gift of peace, we can block it through our own actions. Our hearts will only be troubled if we *allow* them to be troubled.

What is the extent of this peace? Paul tells us in II Thessalonians 3:16.

How does the process work? Philippians 4:6–7 tells us that prayer activates peace. And what peace! It is far beyond anything that anyone can understand. To those who haven't experienced it, seeing it in someone else is astonishing. It doesn't make sense because worldly peace depends on the circumstances. Spiritual peace is focused on an unchanging person: God. That is why it can be present in the worst circumstances, strong and unwavering.

Horatio Spafford experienced the peace of Jesus. A successful lawyer, he was financially ruined by the Great Chicago Fire. Shortly afterward, his only son died. In 1873 he planned to sail to Europe with his family. Delayed by business, he sent his wife and daughters on ahead. The ship encountered disaster. Spafford received a telegram from his wife: "Saved alone." His four daughters had drowned. Spafford immediately booked passage to go to his grieving wife. As his ship passed over the waters where his daughters drowned, he felt moved to write these words:

> When peace like a river attends my way,
> When sorrows like sea billows roll,
> Whatever the cost, thou hast taught me to say,
> It is well, it is well with my soul.

That is peace that transcends understanding. Mary and Joseph would understand.

Question to consider:

Do I have this amazing peace that Jesus gives, or do I choose to block it with anxiety and fear?

Suggested prayer theme: Ask for reminders to bring requests to God with thanksgiving instead of worrying.

Activity choices:

1. Remove Joseph from home. For the rest of this week there will be no action on the set.
2. Music: "It Is Well With My Soul"
3. Decorate with the Noah peace symbol of the dove.

Peace with God

Read Romans 5:11.

So far, we have looked at peace for Israel, a guide for us into the path of peace, marital peace, and personal internal peace that passes all understanding. All of these originate in Christmas. Now we come to the peace that is the basis for all other kinds of peace: peace between God and man.

By taking our sin on the cross, Jesus justified us, and because of this we can be reconciled to God. To reconcile means to restore to friendship, to harmonize apparent opposites.

Remember, Mary considered herself a servant of God, and that was an honor. Because of Jesus's death, we can have the honor only a few had since Adam and Eve left the Garden of Eden: we can be friends with the King. We have become realigned with him, and his ways and thinking, though remaining human. There are your apparent opposites.

Since we are reconciled, we have peace with God. We have returned our allegiance to our true King and he has forgiven us and accepted our fealty. His power has become our protection instead of our vulnerability.

Because we have peace with God, we can petition him with requests instead of worrying, which then results in personal peace. When both spouses have this relationship with God, marital unity results. And when Israel finally accepts her King, she will have peace as well.

The path of peace begins at the cross and leads to the throne of God, and then into the world of relationships. As individuals are reconciled to one another, peace spreads. It could cover the world. Someday it will.

The symbol that reminds me of all this is the calumet or peace pipe. The Native American tribes who used it most used it in two instances: as a seal on a peace treaty, and as part of the adoption ceremony. We have signed a peace treaty with God, and he has declared himself our Father. What could be a more appropriate symbol for peace with God?

Questions to consider:

What does it mean to you to be a friend of God? A child of God?

What difference does it make in your everyday life that you are at peace with God?

Suggested prayer theme: Give thanks and rejoice for reconciliation and peace with God.

Activity choices:

1. Music: "Hark the Herald Angels Sing." Pay extra attention to the first verse.
2. Decorate with peace pipes.

Peace with Others

Read Ephesians 2:11–22.

This peace was quite amazing and at first very disconcerting to the Jews. It took some time to realize they no longer belonged to the only group connected to God, but were now part of an even more special group that included Gentiles. Anyone could join—but most would not.

God took two previously hostile groups of humans, the Jew and the Gentile, combined them, and created a new man. This miracle barely crosses our consciousness today, but it was an enormous feat: a divine feat.

God held out the olive branch to both groups of humanity and in their acceptance of peace with God, they found themselves at peace with each other as friends and brothers. How amazing is that?

Like *Dueling Banjos*, Jews and Gentiles found themselves each playing their own tune, but now in one melodious composition. In today's terms, it would be like Iran and Israel embracing each other as heartfelt brothers. A miracle of peace? Absolutely. Christmas is a time of miracles.

Question to consider:

Is there someone to whom I should be reconciled this Christmas season?

Suggested prayer theme: Ask God which relationships need peace and reconciliation.

Activity choices:

1. Music: "Dueling Banjos"
2. Decorate with olive branches, real or artificial.
3. Music: "They'll Know We Are Christians by Our Love"
4. Become reconciled with those whom God brought to your attention.

Peace on Earth

Read Isaiah 11:1–9.

What else is there to say? That, my friend, is the future, and we'll be there to see it!

There will be peace not only among all humans, but even nature will be returned to its original design, the one lost with the fall of Adam and Eve.

Question to consider:

What draws me most to this future world?

Suggested prayer theme: Pray for the swift return of Jesus.

Activity choices:

1. Music: "Peace in the Valley," including the verse about this future world
2. Decorate with the animals mentioned in the Scripture reading.

   a) Pile together stuffed animals.
   b) Make a parade of stuffed animals lead by a child figure/toy.

c) Make a montage of photos/illustrations of the animals listed in Isaiah.

3. Decorate with the last Noah-related peace symbol: a bow without arrows

   a) Use pictures/illustrations of bows and/or rainbows.
   b) Use a prism that recreates God's rainbow.
   c) Decorate with a real bow hung string side down. This shape, which mimics a rainbow, was a symbol of peace in ancient times. Instead of trying to kill each other with their bows, they hung it up signifying it was no longer needed.

Jesus Loves Us

(Remember, if you are using the Advent Calendar, skip to dated devotions on December 23.)

For today, read Scriptures when you come to them.

How do we know Jesus loved us? He spent a human lifetime with us then died to save us from our sin. It began when Jesus was born of Mary.

Let's be clear about the difference between Jesus's *identity* and his *nature*. Identity is who Jesus is: God. His nature is the entirety of his characteristics.

During the incarnation, Jesus's identity did not change. He always was and always will be God. Jesus claimed deity on many occasions. He talked about God, his Father. He also claimed God's name: *I Am*. The priests handed him to the Romans because the priests judged him blasphemous (Matthew 26: 63–65).

However, during the process of the incarnation, Jesus changed from a God nature to a human nature. His God nature included being all-powerful, all-knowing, present everywhere at the same time, eternal (living out of time), unchanging, and incapable of being tempted (James 1:13).

But according to Philippians 2:6–8 (KJV), Jesus *emptied himself.* Those words are significant. When something is empty there is *nothing* in it. The passage specifically states that it is talking about the nature of God. Jesus emptied himself of it. Now the person who was still God by identity had no God-nature. He had no nature at all.

When Mary became pregnant, Jesus inherited human nature from her. He was a powerless human baby. He knew nothing but what he was taught. He was confined in time and space. Not only was he capable of being tempted, Hebrews 4:15 tells us he was tempted in every way that we are. But he never sinned.

When Jesus was baptized, he received the Holy Spirit just as the few chosen people had received it until then: for a specific mission. It was only after this that Jesus performed miracles. The Holy Spirit was the source of his power and special knowledge.

Jesus did all this because he loved us. He was incarnated because he loved us. He lived the life of a man perfectly in tune with God, and therefore without sin, because he loved us. He showed us the power available to each of us (John 14: 12–13, Matthew 17:20) because he loved us. He died and arose again because he loved us.

It all started with Christmas. No one ever gave us a greater gift.

Question to consider:

Using my small human understanding, what did Jesus give up to be born of Mary?

Suggested prayer theme: Give thanks and adoration for the great love that compelled Jesus to give up so much.

Activity choices:

1. Music: "Love Came Down at Christmas"
2. Music: "Out of the Ivory Palaces"
3. Decorate with rich Christmas red, including adding a red candle to your collection.
4. Decorate with hearts.

The Father Loves Us

Read John 3:16, Romans 5:6–8.

The love of the Father is another part of Christmas. What is there to say? It's incomprehensible. We can hardly understand the story of Abraham nearly offering up Isaac in obedience (Genesis 22), which is an object lesson for us. If you are a parent, you can empathize with Abraham's crisis of faith.

But God designed the plan. He did not sacrifice his son in obedience, but of his own free will. Unlike Abraham, who trusted to the end that God would provide a substitute, God knew that Jesus would die. He knew everything that would happen. And yet, he loved us so much that he gave Jesus anyway. How did the Father feel when Jesus emptied himself, when he died?

Without the Father's great love there would be no Christmas. His love reminds me of the old-fashioned symbol of love: the love knot. It is a knot with no beginning and no ending, like the love of God.

Question to consider:

Have I ever thought about the love of the Father that he showed by creating the plan to save me, and allowing Jesus to fulfill it?

Suggested prayer theme: Give thanks and praise for the Father's amazing love.

Activity choices:

1. Music: "The Love of God"
2. Decorate with love knots or illustrations of love knots.

   a) Make a Swedish Love Knot and hang it up. Directions can be found on the Internet.
   b) Make an Origami Love Knot. Give it to that special someone.
   c) Design your own Love Knot with pen and ink. Hang it as decoration.
   d) Use illustrations of a Love Knot on Christmas cards.

Returning the Love

Read I John 4:19.

Reflecting back the love of God is the other but lesser part of Christmas. Zechariah loved God for his gift—albeit a little late. Elizabeth loved God and became the mother of John. Mary loved God and became the mother of Jesus. Joseph loved God and became not only the husband of Mary, but also the legal father to Jesus. We'll see more love in future devotions.

One of the ways their love for God spilled over was that they just had to tell someone about God's love. Mary told Joseph, Mary and Elizabeth rejoiced together, and even Zechariah got into the act eventually.

This natural spilling over is something we can and should do today.

Questions to consider:

Do I tell others about God's love?

If I do, am I doing it as a duty, or is it a joyous spillover of the flood of God's love? How would each approach be accepted by the one being told?

Suggested prayer theme: Pray to share God's love with joy.

Activity choices:

1. Music: "Pass It On"
2. Decorate with red roses, the symbol of love.

Caesar's Census

Read Luke 2:1

And now we return you to our regular programming: the Christmas story.

Octavius Caesar Augustus was a great military leader and adroit politician. He maneuvered events to retain absolute power in reality while, apparently, restoring the Republic. Essentially, he gave the power to the senate who returned it to him for consecutive terms as Chief Senator until his death. Then they deified him.

The accomplishments of Augustus included restoring the Republic, stabilizing the Empire after decades of civil unrest, imposing the Pax Romana (Roman Peace i.e., peace through force) to the very borders on the west then east, beautifying Rome in marble, building many civic works, supporting the Arts, and raising the morals of the citizens and entertainment.

Now, what about this census? Critics of the Bible have long pointed this out as an error but, of course, it isn't. First, the Bible is an historical book as well as a spiritual one and when *all* the facts are in, the Bible is always proved right. I'll go with those odds any day.

Second, three specific empire-wide censuses have been verified historically, and none of them corresponded to the date of Jesus's birth of 6 or 5 B.C. (Yes, there is a dating error in our calendar.)

Papyri in Egypt described a rolling census. That is, the census rolled through the Empire at regular intervals instead of having one grand Census Day or Census Year. So, the year of the decree was not necessarily the year the census was actually taken in Palestine. Not only that, but in rowdy provinces (and Judah was one!) the census took up to two years to complete.

Besides this, some Roman censuses were taken every fourteen years, but Egypt's was taken every seven years during the reign of Augustus, so possibly the interval was determined province by province. And with Herod the Great on the throne of Israel, Augustus would want to keep close tabs on that kingdom.

Why? First of all, Herod came into disfavor with Augustus in 8-7 B.C. (Interestingly, that was when a 14-year census was due.) Since then, Herod had been treated as a subject rather than a friend with his own vassal kingdom. In fact, people of the time took oaths to both Herod and Augustus, proving Caesar's personal involvement in the province.

Then, too, Herod was insanely paranoid. He was known for repeatedly naming a new heir and then killing him. Augustus would have been aware of this because the changing of Herod's will required Caesar's approval. This was especially important because Herod was ill at the time of the Christmas census, and would die in April of 4 B.C.

And so, God set the stage even to the heart of the Roman Empire, using Caesar Augustus himself, the most powerful man in the world, to play a part in the Christmas story.

Question to consider:

Do I worry about world events and the people in power? Or do I relax, knowing that it is God who is in charge, not human politicians, parties, governments, or militaries?

Suggested prayer theme: Pray for personal peace regardless of the world situation.

Activity choices:

1. Music: "He's Got the Whole World in His Hands" After you sing the common verses, interject the names of world leaders or countries that distress you. Clap your hands. Celebrate God's omnipotence!
2. Decorate with a globe or world map.

Mystery Man

Read Luke 2:2

Luke placed Jesus in a specific time in history. It's almost like he invited his reader to double check his research. Any reader of that time could easily do so. Quirinius was a well-known man.

Critics delight in the fact that, apart from Luke's note, there is no historical proof that Quirinius was governor of Syria at that time. It was a transition year so two governors were named—but not Quirinius. But we do have a historical reference: the detailed research report of Luke, an educated man.

We know from other sources that Quirinius was in Syria at the time with a military expedition. Was he an interim governor and therefore not on the official list? That would certainly nail down the date of Jesus's birth!

For now, we know he was governor of Syria only because of Luke. And that is enough.

Question to consider:

When I come upon unresolved questions in science or history, where do I stand: with human knowledge/theories or with the Bible?

Suggested prayer theme: Give thanks for Biblical accuracy.

Activity:

1.   Music: "The B-I-B-L-E"

Journey to Bethlehem

Read Luke 2:3–5.

The order that "everyone" must return home meant both men and women. There was a head tax on women beginning at twelve years of age and, considering the high death rate in childbirth, a census for that purpose was taken every twelve years. This might even be a reason why the 8–7 B.C. decree was taken in 6 B.C. If the two censuses could be accomplished at the same time, it would save the Empire money and hassle in the troublesome region.

Although critics have declared that people weren't required to return to their clan town, an inscription in 104 A.D. by Vivius Maximus says, "It is essential for all people to return to their homes for the census." While this doesn't prove it happened during the Augustan census, it tells us this was a common practice of the Roman Empire.

Once more, Mary made the long journey from Nazareth in the north, through Perea, and back across the Jordan River into Judea. This time, she had Joseph at her side.

We don't know when the couple started the journey. They had experienced the extensive time it took to complete an Augustan census before. As children, they would have accompanied their parents. Obviously, children could not be left home alone.

Joseph and Mary may have left Nazareth several weeks before she was due. Mary was in her last trimester. The journey was long and tiring. However, the weather would have been pleasant, except in the wasteland around Jericho. There would have little or no rainfall to make her miserable, and temperatures would have been in the seventies.

The couple would have travelled with their extended family from Nazareth for protection from robbers. Did Joseph have children by a previous marriage with him? No. When the Bible records a family doing anything, it specifies children, sometimes by name. There were plenty of other children around, however, to keep the trip merry.

Did Mary ride a donkey? It's highly unlikely. Joseph and Mary were poor and could not afford a donkey. Joseph could have bartered his carpentry skills for the loan of the donkey, but (1) they couldn't afford to feed and lodge it, and (2) they stayed in Bethlehem. How would they have returned the donkey? (3) Also, in Middle Eastern culture, if there was a donkey, the man would ride and the woman walk. Joseph was a godly man, but he was a man of his culture, as well. I think we can rule out a donkey.

Joseph probably brought his tools with him. He would have to provide for his family during the long Census process. Besides, with the town swelling due to the census, there was work available for carpenters. It's also possible that Joseph decided this was a good time to remove Mary from Nazareth gossip permanently. A fresh start would have been appealing.

For whatever reason, they arrived so late, or real estate value had shot up so high due to demand, that Joseph and Mary were unable to stay in a house. For days, maybe weeks, they were forced to live in a stable. What a place to spend Christmas Eve!

Question to consider:

Joseph obeyed the Imperial edict, although he probably chafed under Roman rule. Do I obey the laws of a government I love?

Suggested prayer theme: Pray to be shown any laws I am not honoring.

Activity choices:

1. Attend Christmas Eve service.

    a) Gifts can be placed under the tree while children are at church, if you open presents on Christmas Eve. I prefer the gifts to show up on Christmas Day as representations of the many gifts Jesus brought us through his birth, death, and resurrection.
2. Place Joseph and Mary in Bethlehem, but not in the stable.
3. Music: "Once in Royal David's City"
4. Leave the porch light on for Jesus.
5. You may want to leave milk and cookies for Joseph and Mary instead of Santa Claus.

The following are celebration ideas from other countries. Mix and match, or use a different set each year, or celebrate your own ethnicity.

Alcoholic drinks are included for Christians who drink in good conscience. Christians who do not drink alcohol can substitute any of many Christmas drinks or a non-alcoholic version of the listed drink.

Sweden

1. This is the day to decorate the tree, although it may have been erected earlier.
2. Make braided hearts and other Swedish straw crafts for decoration.
3. Christmas Eve is for the extended family. Everyone can be at one house, or family can visit house to house throughout the day.
4. Keep a coffee table filled with coffee and seven kinds of cookies. They don't have to be the same seven kinds all day. They don't have to be Swedish. They don't have to be homemade. It's the fellowship that is important.
5. Lunch is "dopp i grita" and "glögg."
6. Dinner: Bring it on! Load those tables! Lutfisk is necessary. Rice pudding must contain one almond. The person who finds the almond in his or her serving will have good luck all year.

Germany

1. Children are not allowed in the room while the Christmas tree is decorated.
   a) Use apples, candy, nuts, cookies, toys, tinsel, angels, and lights.
   b) Do not light the lights until Christmas Day.
   c) Put presents under the tree, brought by the Christkind (Christmas angel).
   d) Set a place for each person with fruit, nuts, marzipan, chocolate, and cookies.
   e) Now let the children in!

1. Sing carols around the tree.
2. Celebrate with sparklers.
3. Read the Christmas story.
4. Open gifts in the afternoon.
5. Dinner: suckling pig, carp, or goose served with sausage, macaroni salad, regional dishes.
6. Leave a shoe or boot out to be filled with candy, if you've been good. Otherwise expect twigs.

Ireland

1. Christmas Eve is celebrated at the house of the parents.
2. The emphases:

   a) Welcoming Joseph, Mary, and Jesus.

b) Celebrating with the entire family, including the deceased, since they are alive in heaven.

3. Sweep the floor in preparation for Jesus and his parents.

4. Set a fire in the fireplace to keep them warm.

5. Place green wreaths on graves of family members.

6. Give sweets and apples to children.

7. Celebrate noon with a shotgun blast. (Research your local laws before doing this!)

8. Dinner is the most elaborate meal of the year. It should include spiced beef or boiled ox head or other beef, fowl/poultry, bacon, *and* mutton. Add a variety of puddings and pies.

   a) Christmas Pie is made in the shape of a manger with pastry "boards." If you don't have that shape of pie tin, cut the top crust into a manger shape.

9. Welcome Jesus and his parents with a separate table set for three.

10. Set the table with candles. They will burn from 6 P.M. until midnight.

    a) The largest represents Jesus and is lighted by the youngest child.

    b) Two for Joseph and Mary.

    c) A large candle in a turnip candle holder for each adult in the family.

    d) A smaller candle for each child.

e) Add a candle for each family member who died in the last year.

11. Hang a pillowcase at the end of your bed to be filled by Father Christmas with gifts and sweets while you sleep.

Christmas at Last!

Read Luke 2:6–7.

It's Christmas Day at last! After reading all of these devotionals, do you feel you've been waiting for centuries of prophecy? All those long days of pregnancy with Mary? And now, it's finally here!

I find it humorous that after the extensive description of the conceptions and pregnancies of Elizabeth and Mary, Luke summarizes the birth of Jesus in two sentences. But isn't that just like a doctor? This is a normal human birth: no miracles, no angels, no medical complications. What is there to say, after all?

But let's look at what Luke did say. Jesus was born in Bethlehem while they were there for the census. *The time* could refer to God's timing, or that Jesus was full-term, or both. The birth announcement states that Mary's baby was her first and it was a son. Was it also Joseph's first child? Apparently so. He wouldn't have left the rest of the children in Nazareth.

Swaddling was a common practice not only in Judea but in many places around the world, including Native American nations. The crib was a manger: a dinner table for animals. Traditionally, the stable was a cave. The manger would also have been stone. Today, forests and woodlands cover only 6% of Israel. Even in Jesus's day, many trees were agricultural, such as fig and olive trees, leaving few trees for carpentry, and none for animals.

Was it a silent night? I greatly doubt it. Latecomers were still bustling through town. The town itself was bursting with humanity and animals. Since Mary and Joseph landed in the stable because there was no room in the inn, the odds are that they had lots of company. The stable probably looked like a refugee camp, smelled like it, and sounded like it. Quite possibly, the animals were demoted to the open courtyard. It was pleasant weather and, besides, the stable was wanted for paying guests.

Jesus had come about as low as he could go. He became human. His hometown had a bad reputation. If the future disciple Nathaniel was from my corner of the world, he would have said, "Chicago's South Side? Can anything good come from there?"

Mary had a bad reputation. Joseph and Mary were dirt poor. And, now, Jesus wasn't even born in a clean house!

But Jesus had one thing: Joseph and Mary loved God with all of their hearts and tried their hardest to obey him. They were handpicked by God to love, care for, and teach Jesus.

Question to consider:

How would the world today be different if Jesus had never been born?

Suggested prayer theme: Give thanks and praise for the birth of Jesus. Celebrate!

Activity choices;

1. Place Joseph, Mary, and Jesus in the stable.
2. Set out the tall, fat, white or purple Christ candle, if you haven't already, and light it during devotions, after the other four candles.
3. Place wrapped boxes under the tree or on a table as a centerpiece.

   a) Label each with a gift we receive from God because of the birth of Jesus.
   b) Sign each, "Love, God."

4. Finish your decorating with an explosion of royal purple and gold, sparkles and jewels.

   a) Hang angels in "heaven," place shepherds in the field outside Bethlehem, and place the wise men in their far eastern country.

5. **Now let the kids up!**
6. Go to church.
7. Music: After reading the devotional, enjoy the following in the order listed.

   a) "No Room" from the John Peterson cantata *Night of Miracles*
   b) "Away in a Manger"
   c) "The Birthday of a King"
   d) "Candle on the Water"

      i. Enjoy this while watching the Jesus candle.
      ii. Think of Jesus singing this last song to you.

8. Have a birthday party for Jesus!
9. This is the First Day of Christmas of the Twelve Days of Christmas. The twelve days of Christmas symbolize the long trip of the magi. Set up an area and put in "a partridge in a pear tree." Sing just this verse. Give a gift.

Here are international ideas:

Sweden:

1. Christmas is reserved for the immediate family and for religious celebration.
2. Light candles on graves after church while it is still dark. This is not to worship the dead, but to emphasize that they are not in the graves. The light of Jesus is with them in heaven.
3. Dinner is leftover ham and sausages and bread.

   a) This way, Mom can rest, too!

Ireland:

1. Serve Christmas Cake, which was made in advance.
2. A boy who kisses a girl under the mistletoe must give her a gift.
3. Hunting and shooting matches are held in the afternoon.

4. Spend a quiet evening at home telling stories, holding conversations, singing carols.

England:

1. Decorate with holly, ivy, and mistletoe.
2. Gifts come from Father Christmas and are opened in the afternoon.
3. Dinner: roasted boar's head, turkey, and/or goose, eggnog, roast potatoes, chipolatas, peas, gravy, cranberry sauce, and flaming Plum Pudding.
4. Carry in the wassail ("waes hael" means "good health") bowl ceremoniously.

   a. Accompany it with traditional wassail carols.

Germany:

1. Dinner: roast goose stuffed with apple dressing, and boiled carp with creamed horseradish
2. Goodies include Christollen, Lebkuchen, marzipan, and Dresden Stollen.

Italy:

1. Dinner: roasted capon stuffed with breadcrumbs and sausages, side of grated pecorino.

The Black Sheep Gang

Read Luke 2:8–9.

The shepherds watching the flocks of sheep the night of Jesus's birth were bad dudes. The elders of Jewish towns served as judges of the local population. What were they to do with unruly people? These guys hadn't committed crimes that led to the death penalty. But the elders certainly didn't want them in town! Answer: assign work outside of town and hope they turn into law-abiding citizens. Yeah. That's going to happen.

The Mishna tells us that the sheep these guys were shepherding were destined for temple sacrifice. How appropriate! Jesus had just been born. He would be the ultimate sacrifice for sin. His death would pay for all sin— including all the laws these guys had broken.

So, these guys and their bad reputations lounged around a campfire watching the sheep sleep. One of the Delta Force angels appears out of nowhere! Do you think that grabbed their jaded attention?

At the same time, God's shekinah glory blasted the night all around the shepherds. Remember, this was before electricity. Even to us, this would be a shock. Luke records that it not only got the attention of these tough guys, they were terrified.

What amazing grace! Of all the people on earth, the ones chosen to hear the birth announcement of the Messiah and King were the outcasts of society.

Questions to consider:

Do I reach out to the tough guys and girls of my community, and share the gospel?

Does my church?

Suggested prayer theme: Pray to have God's vision when looking at a tough social outcast.

Activity choices:

1. Hang Gabriel over the shepherds. We don't know this single angel was Gabriel, but since he's the one that gives personal messages about the birth of Jesus, it's a logical guess.
2. Music: "While Shepherds Watched Their Flocks by Night" paying special attention to the first verse
3. Give each child a Shepherd's Staff (candy cane with a hook) and tell them the story of how the candy was invented.

The Story of the Candy Cane

In the 1600s, Christians in Europe began decorating trees as part of their Christmas celebrations. They used cookies and candy for decorations, including white stick candies.

In 1670, the choirmaster at the Cologne Cathedral in Germany bent one end of the stick candies into the form of a shepherd's staff. These were given to children to occupy them during the longwinded sermon on Christmas Day.

This custom spread throughout Europe. The first record of Candy Canes in America was when August Imgard, a German immigrant, used them to decorate his Christmas tree in 1847 in Wooster, Ohio.

Although the Candy Canes were sometimes decorated with red roses, they usually remained white until around 1900. Christmas cards from that time show the candy canes we know today. About this time, peppermint and wintergreen flavors were added to the candy, and have remained the traditional favorites.

Although there is no historical evidence, it is said the shepherd's Staff turned upside down makes a J for Jesus. The red and white stripes represent his blood and purity. There are three stripes which represent the trinity. The hardness of the candy reminds us of the rock of our faith.

International ideas:

England and Germany: Boxing Day

A gift, usually money, is given to each person who serves you during the year, such as the mailman and hair stylist. However, be aware of regulations against gifts to government employees.

England: The second of the Twelve Days of Christmas

Add two turtledoves to your display. Sing the first two stanzas. Give a gift.

<u>Sweden</u>: Annandag Jul

This is the first day of visiting friends, and holding holiday parties. It only makes sense to celebrate a birth *after* it occurred.

Often, several hostesses will get together before Christmas to design a schedule of parties. The plan is to have a party hosted by a different home every night between Annandag Jul and Knut's Day. The biggest parties are on those two days.

Plans for the Annandag Party:

1. Load a snack table with fruits, nuts, chocolates, marzipan, and glögg. Keep it full.
2. Supper: herring, small boiled potatoes, omelet with creamed mushrooms or asparagus, Swedish meatballs, fish loaf with lobster sauce, slices of cod.
3. Dinner: roast pork loin with stewed prunes, creamed vegetables, boiled potatoes, dark ale.
4. Dessert: torte or red berry pudding, or ginger pears with whipped cream.
5. The Ring Cookie Tree is broken among the guests (think communion) and washed down with coffee. Of course, there will be another Ring Cookie Tree at the next party!
6. Sing Christmas carols.
7. Finish with a ringdans around the Christmas tree or a snake dance through the house.

Birth Announcement

Read Luke 2:10–12.

After the usual encouragement not to be frightened, the angel says he brings a message to the shepherds, of all people! It's good news! It has probably been a long time since they've had good news. More than that, it's news of great joy! But it's not just for the shepherds, it's for everyone.

Then follows the birth announcement. When? Today. Where? Bethlehem, the town of David. What? A savior has been born—to you! Then comes the address. It's not "74 King David Road. Turn left at the synagogue. Look for the one-story house with the black shutters." No, the angel tells the shepherds the Messiah is lying in a manger.

There is a tendency for us to think that if a person receives a message straight from God, he or she is a saint in the Catholic sense of the word. This announcement to the Black Sheep Gang certainly disproves that idea! In fact, God contacts people directly when two criteria are met: (1) God wants the person to do something specific, and (2) it is something the person could not find out by reading Scripture. The shepherds fit both criteria.

The message was strange to the ears of the shepherds, but comforting, too. They knew they weren't wanted and they were considered trash. But a manger, like what fed their sheep occasionally, didn't seem threatening. It was something they understood, something within their experience.

But the Messiah born for them? Amazing announcement!

Question to consider:

Do I have the joy of Christmas, or has stress or greed or self-centeredness choked it out?

Suggested prayer theme: Give thanks and praise with joy!

Activity choices:

1. Music: "Amazing Grace"
2. Third day of Christmas: Add three French hens. Sing three stanzas. Give a gift.

Rolling into Town

Read Luke 2:13–16.

As if one Delta Force angel isn't enough to get the message through to these tough shepherds, there is a sudden appearance of many more! The words *host* and *company* were military terms. A host was an army. A Roman company consisted of one hundred soldiers. So a *great company* would have been several hundred Delta Force angels.

Next shock? They start shouting praises to God as if they are in a revival meeting! What's that they say? They (1) glorify God in heaven, and (2) announce peace on earth to men on whom God's favor rests. Who sends warrior angels to declare a peace treaty? God does. Surely, his ways are not like ours.

This peace is not like the Pax Romana, an external enforced peace. It is internal. Unlike the Pax Romana, it is not for everyone, but only for those favored by the Lord. This is the peace beyond understanding that we talked about in an earlier devotional.

After the angels returned to heaven, the shepherds all started talking at once, but they said the same thing: "Let's go see this."

Notice that they believed that the message was from the Lord, and that the birth had happened. These tough guys were way ahead of the priest Zechariah!

The shepherds *hurried* to Bethlehem. Now, I know some of us have visions of cuddly lambs gamboling around the manger. Sorry. Welcome to the real story. Those sheep were nothing more to the shepherds than a way to feed themselves. (Which is why Jesus would later describe himself as the *good* shepherd.)

As for the sheep, they are highly nervous animals. In the middle of the night, they have been shocked by bright light and suddenly appearing angels. Those sheep are long gone: scattered in fear, perhaps dead from shock. The shepherds are in a hurry. They aren't going after the sheep.

What commotion did these guys cause when they came into Bethlehem during the night searching for the manger holding the Messiah? I doubt they quietly moved from stable to stable. It was not in their personality, plus they were in a hurry to find the Messiah. But, sooner or later, they found Jesus and his parents.

Question to consider:

Am I one on whom God's favor rests?

Suggested prayer theme: Pray to learn immediate obedience to the leading of God.

Activity choices:

1. Add the chorus of angels near the shepherds during the devotional reading.
2. After the reading, remove all angels and hurry the shepherds to the stable.

3. Music: "Hark, the Herald Angels Sing"
4. Fourth day of Christmas: Set up four calling birds. Sing four stanzas. Give a gift.

Spreading the Word

Read Luke 2:17–20.

The shepherds had seen the Messiah! What did they do next? They told everyone. Now, they could have seen their reputations as a problem. Shepherds were such notorious liars they were not allowed to testify in a trial. Why would the people of crowded Bethlehem believe them?

The people saw a change in the shepherds. The tough biker gang criminals that came into town now radiated enthusiasm and joy! Their bad attitudes were gone. The subject of their conversations was the Messiah—something unimaginable a mere hour earlier. Even their language was clean. They were glorifying and praising God. And then they responsibly went back to the sheep.

Everyone who heard their message was amazed by it. We don't know how many, if any, went to the stable, but the message of the shepherds was surely the subject of the conversation in every house and around every campfire in town. And when the census was over, the story of strange event would be repeated in the hometowns of the travelers.

Questions to consider:

When I speak to someone of Jesus, am I concerned about their response, which is God's responsibility, or am I concerned with telling as many people as I can?

When I speak of Jesus, am I radiating the joy of the Spirit that is so attractive to others?

Am I joyful about this celebration of Christmas? Is it a real celebration? Or have I made it stressful by including too much work?

Suggested prayer theme: Ask to learn how to witness powered by joy.

Activity choices:

1. Move the shepherds through Bethlehem and back to the fields.
2. Music: "Angels We Have Heard on High"
3. Fifth day of Christmas: Add five "golden" rings. Sing five stanzas. Give a gift.

Officially Jewish

Read Luke 2:21.

Once more Luke is concise. Unlike his extensive description of John's circumcision, Jesus's ceremony is stated in one sentence. Why? Because it was a completely normal event for Jewish boy.

The event was held in either a home or the temple. Most likely, the family stayed in Bethlehem. Which home was used? We don't know. Perhaps the census was over and crowds were gone so the family now lived in a house. Maybe Joseph had built his family a house. Or they may have held the ceremony in the house of the rabbi.

When the ceremony was complete, eight-day-old Jesus was officially a member of the Jewish nation and an heir to the promise. At the same time, he *was* the promise!

Question to consider:

Can I grasp how ordinary this family seemed?

Suggested prayer theme: Give thanks to God for Jesus, the promise.

Activity choices:

1. Music: "There's Something About That Name"

2. Put Joseph, Mary, Jesus, and a "rabbi" in a Bethlehem house.
3. Sixth day of Christmas: Add six "geese a-laying." Sing six stanzas. Give a gift.
4. Pack away shepherds, angels, and the Nazareth set.

Purified and Redeemed

Read Luke 2:22–24.

Joseph and Mary traveled six miles to Jerusalem for these two ceremonies, which were accomplished at the same time. A woman was considered unclean for forty days after the birth of a son. This did not imply that giving birth was sinful. It was related to the issue of blood that occurs normally after childbirth. During this time, the husband could not have sex with his wife. Speaking as a nurse and a woman, I can tell you this ensured a time of adequate healing for the wife.

It's interesting that Luke writes about *their* purification. The Law speaks only of the woman's purification. In this case, the legal father had nothing to do with the conception of the child. Frankly, I don't know why God had Luke write that.

The purification was accomplished by bringing a yearling lamb and a pigeon for the priest to offer on the mother's behalf. If she was too poor to bring that, she could bring two turtledoves or two young pigeons. Mary brought one of these. That's how we know she and Joseph were very poor.

While they were at the temple, they redeemed Jesus. To redeem means to buy back. The first fruits of everything belonged to the Lord, and that included the firstborn son. Instead of leaving Jesus at the temple to serve God, his parents redeemed him, or bought him back, for a shekel. The tribe of Levites served God in the stead of the redeemed boys. And, yet Jesus would serve God and would himself become the Redeemer.

Questions to consider:

Does it make any difference in my life that I have been redeemed at the price of Jesus's death?

What difference will it make during the New Year?

Suggested prayer theme: Ask what difference God wants to see in my life.

Activity choices:

1. Music: "I Will Sing of My Redeemer"
2. Place Joseph, Mary, and Jesus with a priest in the temple.
3. Seventh day of Christmas: Add seven "swans a-swimming." Sing seven stanzas. Give a gift.
4. Put away the inn/stable set, the names of Jesus, and peace week decorations.

Simeon Speaks

Read Luke 2:25–35.

As the scene opens, Simeon is already in Jerusalem. We don't know if he lived there. His qualifications for the job: righteous, devout, waiting for the Messiah, and possessing the Holy Spirit. It seems he was very old because the Spirit assured Simeon that he would not die before seeing the Messiah.

The day Joseph and Mary come to the temple, Simeon follows the prompting of the Spirit to go to the temple courts. Simeon meets Joseph and Mary when they enter. There would have been many people here: men and women, Jews and Gentile converts.

Simeon takes Jesus into his arms and prophesies that this child is the Messiah who would be not only the glory of Israel but also a light to the Gentiles. That last was not an idea expected nor welcomed by Jews. But Simeon wasn't out for popularity.

Joseph and Mary are still having difficulty reconciling Jesus's human nature with his divine identity. He just seems so normal! No halo. No miracles. Just messenger after messenger declaring who he is.

Simeon then blesses Joseph and Mary, which I'm sure they deeply appreciated. It was daunting and depressing to realize one was entrusted with the care of the Messiah.

Simeon tells Mary that Jesus will cause the fall of many self-important people in Israel and raise people from poverty to importance. Obviously, Jesus will not be popular with everyone. The same people who will harm Jesus also will cause Mary extreme pain, foretelling her emotional response to the crucifixion.

And then Simeon walks off the pages of the Bible and, eventually, we can safely assume, into eternity with the righteous.

Question to consider:

When a person meets Jesus, he sees himself as God sees him. Some suddenly realize they are not so very good, so very important, and are brought down. Others realize they have incomparable worth to God, who showers his love on us, and are raised up. Which happened to me when I came face to face with Jesus?

Suggested prayer theme: Pray for insight to see myself as God sees me.

Activity choices:

1. Music: "Open My Eyes That I May See"
2. Eighth day of Christmas: Add eight "maids a-milking." Sing eight stanzas. Give a gift.
3. Pack away Zechariah/Elizabeth/their house and the Love Week decorations except red streamers.

Anna Announces

Read Luke 2:36–38.

Anna was known to everyone in Jerusalem because she was a widow who had lived in the temple for about sixty years. She was eighty-four years old. She was also a prophetess. If she had prophesized for more than several months, it made her the first prophet in four-hundred years. Otherwise, Elizabeth has that honor.

Anna comes up to Joseph's family and Simeon in time to hear Simeon's prophecy. Anna immediately believes and thanks God.

Unlike Simeon, whose ministry is to Joseph and Mary, Anna's assignment is to announce the Messiah to people in the temple. She does not waste the news on those who are only in the temple because of duty or for show. After all the years spent there, Anna knows which people are truly looking for the Messiah. She makes a beeline for them.

It doesn't say how long she did this. From what little we know of Anna; I think she announced the Messiah every day in the temple for the rest of her life.

Question to consider:

While I go through my days, do I listen for people who are open to the gospel, or am I intent on accomplishing my own goals?

Suggested prayer theme: Pray to be attuned to the spiritual openness of others.

Activity choices:

1. Music: "List Our Merry Carol" or "Masters In This Hall"
2. Ninth day of Christmas: Add nine ladies dancing. Sing nine stanzas. Give a gift.
3. Pack away the bells.

Stellar Announcement

Read Matthew 2:1–2.

Today, we are switching from Luke's emphasis on the humanity of Jesus to Matthew's emphasis on Jesus as Messiah and King. It is fitting that Matthew wrote the gospel containing the account of the magi.

The magi may have been minor or vassal kings. They visited Herod the Great, king of Palestine under Roman rule looking for King Jesus. How much royalty can be squeezed into one story?

What the King James Version translates as "kings" is interpreted by most other versions as "magi." Magi were priests of Zoroastrianism. According to this religion, each person has a "star-double."

They were wealthy aristocrats, learned in medicine, natural sciences, astrology, and alchemy. The last two were considered sciences on the same level as biology and chemistry at that time.

So, we have educated priests (maybe kings as well) who came to Jerusalem for an audience with King Herod. Why? I mean, why Jerusalem? Jesus was born in Bethlehem. Let me suggest some possibilities.

- As important visitors from a foreign country, it was politically necessary to make a state visit to the local king.
- Historians writing at that time recorded that people all over the Middle East were looking for a messiah at that time, although not necessarily in the Jewish meaning of the word. Something about the star seen by the magi was so extraordinary that it sent them to research and then on a long, dangerous journey looking for the star's human "double."
- Jews had lived "in the East" since Palestine was sacked centuries earlier. Some Jews returned to Palestine eventually, but some did not or could not. These exiles had contributed to the knowledge of the Parthian Empire with their holy books and teachings. The magi, as learned men, probably knew Numbers 24:17. Logically, that would point them toward Palestine.
- Because of the prophecy, they knew they were looking for a king. The logical place to find the new King of the Jews was Jerusalem. They assumed this messiah was Herod's son. In the next devotional, you will see how ludicrous this was, but they came anyway.
- They had no other directions. The magi reported to Herod they had seen the star "in the east." That was all. They did not follow a star to Jerusalem.

The star got their attention. After that, their priestly interest, scholarly research skills, and even their own false religion gave them clues to follow to the logical end: Jerusalem and King Herod.

Questions to consider:

How familiar am I with Biblical prophecy for the next coming of Jesus?

If God directed me to do something that would upend my life, perhaps even something dangerous, would I do it? Would my obedience be immediate and enthusiastic?

Suggested prayer theme: Pray for obedience like the magi.

Activity choices:

1. Put away Simeon, Anna, the temple, and yellow streamers and bunting.
2. Move Joseph, Mary, and Jesus to their house in Bethlehem.
3. Remove the star from "the east" then move the wise men to Herod's palace in Jerusalem.
4. Music: "One Fair Morn" also known as "The March of the Kings"
5. (Of course, this is a Middle Ages romantic interpretation, like all Christmas traditions, but you can get an idea of the enormous entourage the magi would have brought.)
6. Decorate with royal purple bunting and/or streamers.
7. Write an article for the *Jerusalem Times* newspaper about the arrival of the magi. It could be hard news, an editorial, or a society/gossip column. If more

than one person participates in this, you could put out an entire newspaper!

8. Tenth day of Christmas: Add ten "lords a-leaping." Sing ten stanzas. Give a gift.

When Herod Ain't Happy

Read Matthew 2:3.

A paraphrase could be, "When Herod ain't happy, ain't nobody happy." But why was Herod *disturbed*?

1. The appearance of the magi. Herod's kingdom and nearby lands were craved by both the Roman Empire on the west and the Parthian Empire to the east because important trade routes snaked through these lands. Indeed, Parthia had invaded Judea in 18 B.C. and had sent Herod running for his life to the safety of Rome. This visit by the magi occurred in 5 or early 4 B.C. The indignity of the Parthian invasion was still fresh in Herod's paranoid mind. Why were the magi really here? Were they spies sent to scout weakness for another invasion?

2. Their message of a new King of the Jews. Herod claimed that title and he knew he'd fathered no son recently. Who was this king? Was this another threat to his throne? And how could he be *born* king? One was born a prince and crowned a king. How fortunate the magi had come to him! Forewarned is forearmed.

3.	The magi's desire to worship this king. Herod was keenly aware that kings as a rule—himself included—were not worshipped. Gods were worshipped. At this time Caesar Augustus had not yet been deified, so that was not on Herod's mind. I'm not sure what he was thinking except if foreign dignitaries had come to worship this King of the Jews, his own throne was in serious jeopardy!

That covers Herod. But why was all of Jerusalem disturbed? Could it be because Herod the Great was an unstable paranoid psychopath with extensive power? Yes, I think that would do it. When Herod is disturbed (such an ironic understatement and double meaning!) everyone around him is terrified for their lives. And that's no exaggeration.

If you want to know why, read his history below.

48 B.C. Herod is appointed governor of Galilee when he is twenty-five years old by his father, Antipatar.

43 B.C. Father offers financial support to Caesar's murderers. He's poisoned. (Herod?)
Herod executes his father's murderers, backed by the Roman Army.

39-37 B.C. Nephew Antigonus tries to usurp the throne, but is defeated and executed by Marc Antony. Herod banishes his first wife, Doris, and their three-year-old son, Antipater. Then, he marries his teenage niece, Mariamne.

36 B.C. Herod fears the Jews will appoint his seventeen-year-old brother-in-law, Aristobaulus III, as King of the Jews, so Herod appoints his nephew High Priest.

35 B.C. Aristobaulus III is drowned at a party, on Herod's orders.

31 B.C. Octavian defeats Mark Antony and declares himself Caesar. Herod switches allegiance to Octavian (Caesar Augustus).

30 B.C. Caesar Augustus confirms Herod as King of Judea.

29 B.C. Herod's passion and jealousy for Mariamne results in charging her with adultery. His sister is the chief witness. Mariamne's mother, hearing she's on the list for execution, testifies against her daughter. Mariamne is executed. Her mother declares herself Queen on the basis that Herod is morally unfit to serve. Big mistake. She is executed without a trial.

28 B.C. Herod executes his brother-in-law for conspiracy.

27 B.C. An assassination attempt on Herod is foiled.

23 B.C. Herod marries his third wife, also named Mariamne, daughter of the high priest, Simon. She is the third of ten wives.

18 B.C. Herod runs for his life when the Parthian Empire invades Judea. He returns the same year after Rome recaptures the land.

7 B.C. Herod executes his two sons by Mariamne for conspiring to kill him. Caesar has serious doubts about Herod and demotes him from independent ruler to co-ruler, making Herod a vassal king of Rome.

5 B.C. Herod is seriously ill with chronic kidney disease complicated with Fournier's gangrene.

5 or 4 B.C.   The magi arrive.

4 B.C. Jewish zealots smash the golden eagle of Rome over the main entrance of Herod's Temple. Herod executes his oldest son for conspiring to kill him. The joke around Judea is that "It is safer to be Herod's pig than his son."

Herod dies in April.

Questions to consider:

The gossip mill is working overtime, which is how all of Jerusalem knows to be afraid. Isn't it interesting that God even used gossip to get the word out about the birth of Jesus? Do I believe God can turn anything to good?

Suggested prayer theme: Praise God that he is all-knowing.

Activity choices:

1. Decorate with crowns.
2. Put away inside candles including the Advent Wreath or candle arrangement. You may want to leave out the Jesus candle.
3. The only song that describes King Herod and his effect on people is "They're Coming to Take Me Away." If that's sacrilegious to you, don't use it. But when I listen to the madness behind the words and envision myself as a Jew under Herod's nearly limitless authority, it terrifies me. I understand this story at gut level.

4. Eleventh day of Christmas: Add eleven pipers piping. Sing eleven stanzas. Give a gift.

Herod's Last Chance

Read Matthew 2:4–8.

Why didn't God use the star to lead the magi directly to Bethlehem? We aren't told in the Bible, but it would be just like God to give even Herod one last chance.

Herod must know he's dying. Will he finally choose God and be cleansed of all the sins in his evil life? Will he go with the magi and worship someone besides himself? Will he acknowledge a higher king?

Herod had just enough Jewish teaching to realize he is dealing here with the Messiah although he, like most Jews, understood the Christ as a physical king—and now a personal threat. Herod has one pattern for dealing with threats: kill them. He intentionally sets out to kill the prophesied Messiah.

His first step is to call *all* of the experts on the Law. Herod was thorough. He didn't want to miss the one who might have the piece of information he sought. Herod, himself, doesn't know Scripture well enough to know the answer, so he gets it from the experts.

During this time, Herod is probably attempting to impress the magi with the opulence and hospitality of his kingdom in the extravagant Middle Eastern tradition. After hearing from the experts, Herod calls the magi to a *secret* conference and asks them for the exact time the star appeared in the east. Why? Because it was a birth star and would tell Herod the age of the child.

Since he used this information to determine the age of the children to be killed in Bethlehem in the massacre to be two years and younger, I think Jesus was probably about one year old at the time of the Jerusalem visit of the magi. That places him squarely in the middle of Herod's safety net of calculations.

Of course, Herod doesn't tell the magi what's in his mind. He says this:

1. Go. They had permission to leave and travel through his kingdom.
2. They are to make a *careful* search, a painstaking search, and leave no stone unturned, no home unsearched. Note that Jesus is referred to as a child, not a baby nor infant.
3. They are to report back immediately. There is urgency here. The clock is ticking.

The reason that Herod gives is that he intends to worship the child, too. Do the magi believe him? Perhaps, but I doubt it. They were probably aware of Herod's reputation. A secret meeting would reinforce that. However, if they didn't agree, they probably would have met with an unfortunate accident.

Questions to consider:

How do I feel about Herod? Am I disgusted with his chicanery? Am I angry that he intends to kill Jesus? Of am

I sad that he has thrown away what may have been his last chance of salvation? How do I think God felt at this time?

Suggested prayer theme: With God's heart, pray for one world leader, political or religious, that actively tries to kill Americans or is involved in ethnic cleansing or Christian persecution within his own country.

Activity choices:

1. Music: "Go and Search Diligently" from John Peterson's cantata *Night of Miracles*.
2. Twelfth day of Christmas: Add twelve drummers drumming. Sing the entire song. (Can you do it in one breath?) Give a gift.
3. Turn off/remove outdoor holiday lighting.

Gifts Fit for a King

Read Matthew 2:9–12.

What a peculiar star!

It was so unusual in some way that the magi recognized that it signified the birth of an important person. It gave them the direction to search. Then it disappeared.

It may have been visible only the night of Jesus's birth. It may have been visible only to the magi who were receptive to the message. Was it visible by day? We don't know.

After leaving Herod, the magi saw the same star again, even though they were now in the west. The star *went ahead of them* and the magi followed. The star travelled south. Remember, it's only six miles to Bethlehem, and yet, the star was seen as moving. Its destination was not over the town in general, but specifically over the house where Mary and Jesus were. I have no idea what that means, but its behavior is like no star I've ever seen or heard of!

Skeptics try to explain away the star. They want it to be the conjunction of Jupiter, Saturn, and Mars that occurred in 6 B.C. or a nova. Besides the fact that neither of them fit the description of events, the magi were learned in astronomy—though they tended to mix it with astrology. They would be familiar with conjunctions and novas even if they didn't understand them. Anything ordinary in the sky wouldn't make an impression sufficient to send them on a long, dangerous journey.

Can you imagine the scene when the magi and their entourage entered Bethlehem?

Can you imagine living in a small town when the presidential limousine and a protection detail enters the narrow main street? You probably drop what you're doing to follow it: you and everyone in town!

You see the caravan stop at the house of Joseph and Mary. What in the world is going on? The Secret Service takes a quick reconnaissance and moves the crowd back. One of them opens the door of the limousine and... I'm sure you get the picture.

Can you imagine being Mary? (We don't know where Joseph was. Maybe he was out on a job.) You hear a commotion and hurry to the door just in time to see the caravan stop at your door. Stunned, you hurry to provide refreshments, but you hear the call for permission to enter.

The magi enter and bow to the little King (with no particular attention made to Mary). The magi worship him. Then they open the gifts they had brought the King. We don't know how many magi there were. We don't know how many and what kind of gifts they brought. We do know they brought three gifts of enough significance to be mentioned in the Bible.

The first gift was gold. Gold was a gift given to kings. Indeed, no one but kings and wealthy people could afford to own gold. This gift was the acknowledgment of the magi that Jesus was King of the Jews.

The second gift was frankincense. This resin of the Boswellia tree is associated with worship. The gift recognized Jesus as God.

The third gift was myrrh. This is resin from a small thorny tree. It is associated with pain, death, and sacrifice. It recognized Jesus as Savior. Myrrh was mixed with vinegar and offered to Jesus on the cross to ease his pain. It was used by Joseph of Arimathea to anoint the body of Jesus after death.

Did the magi know the significance of their gifts? There is no way to know. But we do know they speak to us.

Question to consider:

What specific examples show that my life reflects my belief that Jesus is King, God, and Savior?

Suggested prayer theme: Request the Holy Spirit's assistance to obey Jesus as King, worship him as God, and thank him as Savior.

Activity choices:

1. Music:
   a. "When They Saw The Star" from John Peterson's cantata *Night of Miracles*
   b. "We Three Kings of Orient Are"

1. Display gold, frankincense, and myrrh.
2. Deliver the baby items you've collected to the intended charity.

3. Have one final feast. Include anything shaped like a star or crown such as Crown Cake, star cookies, star fruit.
4. After the children are in bed, pack away the remaining seasonal items.

Sweden

1. Deliver gifts to friends while carrying a star wand.
2. Pack away the purple and gold items, the rest of the nativity set, and the Jesus candle.
3. Parties will continue daily until Knutdagen (Knut's Day).

Germany

1. Deliver gifts to friends while carrying a star wand.
2. Take a long walk to commemorate the long journey of the magi. Traditionally, this would be to church on Epiphany Sunday.

Italy

1. Christmas gifts are given today. Even if you aren't Italian, I'm sure the children would appreciate one more gift to commemorate the gifts of the wise men.

Nicholas's Day December 6

Read I Timothy 6:17–19.

Nicholas was a church leader who was born in the year 270. What year is it now? Wow! That was a long time ago!

Nicholas was known for his kindness and generosity. Those are things we should be, too.

Let me tell you the most famous story about Nicholas. We don't know if it is true.

Nicholas heard that the daughter of a very poor man was old enough to be married. In those days, the girl was expected to bring a dowry to the marriage: money or property usually. Without a dowry, the girl was doomed to whatever man would have her. These men were usually bad men and often criminals. They were not the kind of man a Christian girl should marry.

The father was so worried! What if the man beat his daughter?

Nicholas was a rich young man at the time. The night after he heard the story, Nicholas crawled onto the family's roof and dropped a bag of gold down the chimney.

The kitchen fireplace had a four-foot square opening with hooks to hold the handles of cooking pots. At night, the fire was allowed to die down and laundry was hung on the hooks.

The bag of gold fell into one of the daughter's stockings she had hung to dry!

Oh, the father and daughter were happy! They laughed and danced around the house. Now, the father was able to arrange for a marriage for his daughter with a kind Christian man.

Nicholas did the same for the second daughter. The night he threw gold down for the third daughter, the father had hidden himself. He caught Nicholas. Nicholas begged the father not to tell, but somehow the story came out.

Question to consider:

I may not be able to give bags of gold to the needy, but I can give some amount of money, time, and love. Do I need to be more generous?

Suggested prayer theme: Request a generous heart

Activities:

1. Decorate with Nicholas, not Santa Claus. Omit Santa Claus movies, visits, etc.
2. A nearby city may have a Nicholas Day celebration to attend.
3. Play a game of throwing a beanbag or rock into your Christmas stocking.
4. Hang your stocking. Do it at the fireplace if you have one. This is done December 5.
5. Fill stockings during night with candy and small gifts. Include gold foil wrapped candy.

6. I allowed my kids to open one big gift with the stocking. It took the anticipatory edge off their emotions and gave them one new toy to play with.

7. Someone could dress as Nicholas and visit the family. Perhaps he could bring with him the one gift for each child.

8. Set out the candy and nuts for browsing and keep bowls filled.

9. In Germany, Nicholas brings all of the gifts on November 6.

Lucia's Day December 13

Read John 8:12, Matthew 5:14–16.

Lucia was an Italian girl born into a wealthy family. The stories of her life vary but they all agree she became a Christian when a child, probably through her nurse (nanny).

The most oft-told story is that Lucia's mother became sick. While praying for her mother, Lucia vowed to give her wedding dowry to the church if her mother recovered. The mother revived and Lucia paid her vow.

However, this did not sit well with her fiancé who considered the money his. In his rage, he told the soldiers of Emperor Diocletian that Lucia was a Christian. This meant her death. The soldiers tried to burn her at the stake, but the flames blew away from her. In exasperation, Lucia's fiancé thrust his sword through her heart.

Lucia is thought of in connection with light because of the bonfire of her death and because she tried urgently to convert her family and friends to Jesus, the Light of the World. Also, by the old calendar, Lucia Day fell on the shortest day of the year: the day that brought increasing light to the cold Nordic lands.

Question to consider:

Do I tell my friends about Jesus, the Light of the World?

Suggested prayer theme: Pray for courage and love to tell others about Jesus

Activities:

In <u>Germany</u>, miniature replicas of the family home are fitted with four stained "glass" windows and a candle behind each window. At nightfall, the candles are lit and the houses are set in the river, which carries them bobbing down the current—or capsizes them.

Sweden:

1. Decorate with lights and candles in windows and everywhere. Decorate with goats, Dala horses, Swedish straw ornaments, and Lucy figures.
2. Breakfast is made and served by the oldest daughter. (Some say youngest, but most sources agree on oldest.) Breakfast traditionally consists of coffee and Lucia Buns, but you can modify this to the tastes of your family. "Lucia" serves breakfast in bed to each family member while singing *Sancta Lucia*, preferably in Swedish. Or she can hum it.

    "Lucia" wears a long white robe with a red sash, red stocking or bare feet, no shoes, and a candle wreath on her head. Although real candles are traditional, battery candle wreaths are available and recommended.

3. In Sweden, "Lucia" visits unfortunates in hospitals, nursing homes, orphanages, and jails with coffee and Swedish cookies.

Notes:

I had my oldest daughter play Lucia. I presented it as an honor, which it is. She was always proud that it was her right. Her younger sister missed her sister when she grew up and moved, but was happy that she could now play Lucia.

We attend a local Swedish Lutheran Church for a traditional Lucia Service on the Sunday closest to Lucia Day.

Knut's Day January 13

Read Psalm 24:7–10.

King Knut (also spelled Canute, Cnut, Knute) was a Danish king of the eleventh century who added Norway, parts of Sweden, and all of England to his empire. He made England the base of his kingdom.

Although a Viking, Knut was a Christian. Tradition says he declared, "We extend the celebration of Christmas to twenty days. My son's birth was celebrated for a fortnight. It is only right that the birth of the King of Kings be celebrated longer."

This set the end of Christmas on January 6: Twelfth Night or Three Kings Day. However, when a new calendar began to be used in the seventeenth century, Knut Day landed on January 13.

The Swedes, who are the only ones to celebrate this day today, joyfully throw parties for an extra week, with the biggest party saved for Knut Day. In fact, in some parts of Sweden, especially in Uppland province, north of Stockholm, the people celebrate with carnivals!

I love the idea of Christmas going out with a bang!

Question to consider:

Do I really understand the implications of Jesus as King of Kings?

Suggested prayer theme: Request to learn proper respect for my brother-king Jesus, and my Father God.

Activities: Knut's Day party

Preparation:

1. Decide whom you will invite. Traditionally, the extended family is invited, especially the children. You may decide to invite disadvantaged children of your church or community.
2. Decide where to hold the party, who will host it (more than one person may host the same party), what activities will be included, and who is responsible for what.
3. Decide if a dinner or smorgasbord (buffet) will be served. Each guest can be invited to bring any remaining Christmas food or drink. The rule is: All Christmas food and drink must be finished on Knut Day!
4. If you are having the party in your home, put all decorations away including all Christmas tree decorations. Decorate the tree completely with edibles: popcorn balls, gum stick "icicles," popcorn garlands (colored popcorn is great!), candy, nuts, fruit.

Party Fun:

1. Welcome your guests. Tell them no one is to touch the tree until permission is given at the end of the party.
2. Begin dinner or open the smorgasbord

   a. A toast (can be non-alcoholic) to King Jesus followed by three cheers
   b. The story of Knut Day followed by a toast to King Knut.
   c. A special welcome to children
   d. Luke 18:16–17 followed by prayer over the food.
   e. Remind everyone that all food and drink must be consumed today!
   f. Dig in!

3. Games for everyone, especially for the children
4. At the end of the party, the children "rob the tree." It's good to set down rules.

   a. You may rob the tree on the word "go." (1,2,3, go)
   b. Take only what is in front of you. This will let taller kids take candy only they can reach, leaving middle tree goodies for shorter children, and the lowest branches for toddlers and preschoolers, who will be much slower and otherwise might not get much.

c. Anyone who pushes someone else away, grabs goodies of another, upsets the tree or causes someone else to upset the tree is immediately barred from further participation.

5. When the tree is bare, finish the party with "att dansa julen ut" (all dance Christmas out). Ringdans around the tree to Swedish Christmas music then dance the tree out of the house with a snake dance. One more dance around the tree and Christmas is over for another year. (If you don't have Swedish Christmas music, "O Christmas Tree" is a good substitute although it's stately rather than bouncy.)

After the Party:

1. If you are going to plant a live tree, take it to the garage. Artificial trees should also be disassembled outside of the house. A cut tree can be chopped and used in the house fireplace in the coming days as a reminder to live the truths of Christmas in our hearts all year.
2. If the food and drink wasn't finished during the party, take them to some worthy cause where they will be consumed today: a food pantry, a nursing home, the Sheriff's Department.
3. Consider these questions: When I think about the children at the party, what does their behavior teach me about how I should receive the kingdom of God? Do I need to fix my attitude or priorities?

Note:

January 13 is the date for Knut's Day by the old Nordic calendar and the date it is celebrated today. In our calendar, Knut's Day falls on January 6: Three Kings Day. It is probable that the Twelve Days of Christmas began with King Knut's proclamation. If you choose, you could have the Knut Day party on January 6.